Mary's Prayer

Mary McGuinness

BALBOA.
PRESS
A DIVISION OF HAY HOUSE

Balboa Press books may be ordered through booksellers or by contacting:

Balboa Press
A Division of Hay House
1663 Liberty Drive
Bloomington, IN 47403
www.balboapress.com
1 (877) 407-4847

Printed in the United States of America.

ISBN: 978-1-4525-2071-1 (sc)
ISBN: 978-1-4525-2072-8 (hc)
ISBN: 978-1-4525-2073-5 (e)

Library of Congress Control Number: 2014914835

Balboa Press rev. date: 10/02/2014

This book is written for the invisible people of our society, who have suffered in silence, too afraid to bear their soul, in case others derided them for their weakness and lack of character. It is also for those members of the community who are considered a liability to everyone because they are unable to work and contribute to society. Furthermore, it is for people who suffer yet somehow continue to function but that they find life very difficult, yet never find themselves in the system.

Life is what happens to you while
you're busy making other plans.
—John Lennon, 1980
"Beautiful Boy", *Double Fantasy*

Contents

PART I

The Past Is Myself

PART II

Universal Problems

PART III

Solutions

PART IV

Moving Forward

Foreword

There remains, for most of us, the darkness wherein anxieties become fears, fears which are realised and developed in the obscurity we cannot pierce. They paralyse us. Since we cannot see out, we have to seek within for that flicker of faith, hope, or inspiration which can furnish sufficient light for a single step. And then another, sometimes the step will be faltering or require to be retraced. Yet we shall be moving on, gaining enough self-sufficient knowledge to illuminate the way.

—Benny Timpson
Mentor on *Mary's Prayer*

Preface

S ince 2008, I have contemplated writing a self-help book for people who found themselves in the same situation as I. Suffering from any form of depression is difficult for many people to understand, and the stigma associated with the illness still exists today. During my own quest for answers, I constantly met obstacles which I hope people will avoid after reading *Mary's Prayer.*

The concept of *Mary's Prayer* was developed several years ago when I visited Lourdes, France; however, I started to write the book two years ago. Writing this book has taken me on a spiritual journey to find inner peace. My faith has grown over the years, particularly since I visited the shrine of Lourdes and the church of Frauenkirche in Munich, where I believe I received a blessing. In Lourdes, I was struck by the nightly processions and the recitations of the Rosary. The pilgrims there were very ill, and yet they had this great devotion to Our Lady. My visit to the Marian shrines made a major impact on my life, one that was pivotal in helping me change direction.

Having read many self-help books over the last few years, I couldn't seem to access the information that was applicable to my life story. There were many stories written by family members but few by the survivors themselves. Initially I was reluctant to share my story with family and friends, but as the years went by, I realised that perhaps the only way to change opinions was to be truthful about what had happened to me.

I was encouraged to write after reading Terri Cheney's book, *Manic*. I was also impressed by the film, *The Way* (Estevez 2011). Perhaps the book *Eat, Pray, Love* by Elizabeth Gilbert was my greatest inspiration, although the fact that part of my recollections are based in Italy is the only parallel to that story. I also loved the film of the same name (Murphy 2011). Transformation of the protagonists takes place in both of these films, and I also lived similar experiences through the journey within myself to look for answers to my problems.

Studying for a degree in psychology was instrumental on the road to attaining peace of mind. There were elements of the course which provided solutions and reasons for why I had become ill. Although clinical psychology was not part of the course, I found other eminent psychologists had actually offered solutions in their work. In particular, social construction theory, humanistic psychology, and social psychology in general greatly impacted on this book.

Music has been a particular source of comfort throughout my life. The Beatles were a great influence from an early age, and John Lennon's lyrics made me realise that I was not alone in the way I was thinking. I identified with John Lennon, especially during the five-year period he spent away from the music business, prior to the release of *Double Fantasy* in 1980.

The song "Watching the Wheels" has always made me feel that someone understood how it felt to stop working. Liverpool has become important to me over the last three years. Travelling in Europe had been a favourite pastime until I was affected by illness in 2000. These memories of Italy and Munich in particular have helped me through many difficult years.

It is only when you are in a situation that you learn how to deal with it. Many people might wonder how I managed to survive the years of isolation when my life had been very different. I took each day at a time, and eventually I moved on from the past.

One of the reasons I wrote *Mary's Prayer* was because I finally found peace myself, and I believed it is possible for others to achieve this state of mind by following my example. The inscription on the Peace and Harmony statue on the cover of *Mary's Prayer* reads "Peace on Earth" and "The Conservation of Life", which is the message of this book. Peace is essential within each of us. Because of our spiritual connection with others on Earth, peace should be attainable throughout the world.

After the film *The Secret* was released in 2007, I became interested in the Law of Attraction (R. Byrne 2006). The metaphysics of this law states that we are all energy and we operate at different frequencies. It simply harnesses the ability to tune into the higher-frequency states, which allows this law to attract good things into your life. The emphasis is on having good thoughts and vibrations. The highest-energy state is that of love. I believe that this may offer some solution to the low-energy states that exist in depressive conditions.

Along the journey, I met various people, including Lilia Sinclair and Karyn Klapecki, who introduced me to the Sedona Method. Christine McGrory's *The Key* also helped move me forward, thanks to meeting people with a similar interest in the Law of Attraction. I also found Brandon Bays's *The Journey* very helpful.

Mary's Prayer came into being as the title, thanks to Gary Clark from the Scottish band Danny Wilson, who wrote a song of the same name in 1988. The lyrics of the song had resonated with me since that time and became poignant years later.

I hope to be able to campaign now for people who find themselves in a similar situation.

Acknowledgements

T hanks to my parents, whose support has been essential throughout my life.

Many thanks to my sister, Lena for her friendship, love and loyalty throughout the years Also I thank Lena for charting our travels with her excellent photography, as she has provided most of the photos for this book.

I have great gratitude for the expert advice I received from the team at Balboa press.

Thanks to Kathy Milligan for her support through the years.

A special thanks to Gary Clark for composing "Mary's Prayer" which was a great comfort to me since 1988 and for his permission to entitle this book with the same name. Also thanks to Kit Clark and Ged Grimes (both formerly of Danny Wilson).

Thanks to Dr John V. Docherty, whose support in the last fifteen years has helped me through very difficult times.

Thanks to Benny Timpson, my former English teacher, who became involved with *Mary's Prayer* just over a year ago. His advice and expertise have been pivotal in the development of *Mary's Prayer.* He has also been a great mentor and friend.

Many thanks to my great friend, Elina Milano for her continual support, love and friendship.

A special thanks to Gail Renard for her friendship.

Thanks to Antonio Piedra for his friendship,wisdom and encouragement with "Mary's Prayer"

Thanks to Aina, Lars and Family.

Thanks to Gerard Durkan.

Thanks to Lilia Sinclair and Christine McGrory.

Thanks to Anne and Gary Macleod.

Thanks to Arvid Breitenbach; my great friend of many years.

And finally, thanks to Kevin and Julie Roach for their love and support throughout the last few years.

PART I

The Past Is Myself

Introduction

T his book focuses on how my life was affected by the breakdowns of my health and the subsequent recoveries over a fourteen-year period from 1999 until 2013. After each breakdown, I had to learn to be patient until my health improved. It was a long journey, and in the early stages, I could not concentrate to read, so I listened to music or the radio until this time passed that I could resume these activities.

Through reading the book, *The Secret,* I became interested in the healing aspect of the Law of Attraction. I formulated a method by which I could recover, should I ever become ill again. Music, literature, and movies were important to me throughout that period, as I was isolated because of illness and my financial situation. I listened mainly to John Lennon's music and the Beatles during that period. I became interested in the success coaches in America; particularly in Jack Canfield, Bob Proctor and Jack Black here in the United Kingdom. Eventually I studied for a degree in psychology with the Open University.

I had qualified as a chartered accountant in 1994, and finding work thereafter was an uphill struggle. For two years after qualifying, I worked on a contract basis until I found permanent work. After my first period of illness, I was advised by medical professionals to change careers. This was difficult, as my work was my life at the time, and I could not see the way forward. It was traumatic, as I had expected to work in this field for the rest of my life.

The approach to this work is autobiographical, and the second part of the book is topical, as I explain ways I found to change my life. The reader should realise that even when the odds are stacked against you, it is possible to move forward and take action to change the course of your life. I personally was very fortunate to graduate from Glasgow University, Heriot Watt University and qualify as a chartered accountant prior to this illness. Even after the period of illness in 2008, I still could motivate myself to study for a degree in psychology. I hope this book gives insight into an illness which is so stigmatised that people rarely speak about it. Perhaps one of the most difficult aspects of the illness is that there is little sympathy for it, unlike physical illnesses, and a lack of understanding from the majority of people.

CHAPTER

Growing Up

I was born in the summer of 1966 in Coatbridge in central Scotland. The town itself had become popular with immigrants from Northern Ireland looking for work. Coatbridge had been important during the Industrial Revolution, with the ironworks, mining works, steel works, and many factories. My great-grandparents moved here from Northern Ireland at the turn of the twentieth century to make a better life for their families. Education was always important to improve our circumstances.

Mine was a happy childhood, being part of a large extended family. My father worked in the construction business, and my mother was a housewife. Lena, my sister, was my guiding light from an early age. We lived in the same street as my maternal grandmother, in close proximity to my aunts, uncles and their families. My grandmother's house was the meeting point for the relatives. I was the youngest on the maternal side of the family amongst the cousins. My parents were both the second youngest in their families. Therefore, many of my cousins were much older than I. Many of my uncles had served in the Second World War, and we heard the stories of where they travelled and how important it was to them while they were fighting to know they had a family back home.

I started St Patrick's Primary School in August 1971. A whole new world opened up for me there. I loved learning and meeting new friends from the other side of town. The teachers were inspirational, and they prepared us for life. Education was very important to me, and I had a natural aptitude for many subjects. After my homework was done, I loved to play at the nearby park. Every Sunday, we visited my paternal grandparents, who lived about four miles from Coatbridge; we met up with the rest of the family there.

The summer holidays of my childhood were spent every year in Blackpool, on the North-West coast of England. Before the package holidays to Spain in the 1970s, many people from the area in which I lived travelled there during the Glasgow Fair Fortnight, which was held in the middle of July. The weather was good in those days, and even if it rained in Blackpool, there was enough entertainment to keep us happy. The Pleasure Beach, the amusement arcades, the Winter Gardens where the Beatles played years earlier and the Opera House were great places to visit. The town had a seven-mile promenade and three Victorian piers with lots of entertainment all year round. Many of my cousins and their parents travelled with us to Blackpool. There were always lots of people around me, and as a result, I made friends easily.

My maternal grandmother died in June 1974, just before my eighth birthday. On reflection, this must have made a tremendous impact on my life, as I had spent a lot of time with her. Before my grandmother died, she gave me her prayer book, which had been a gift to her from one of my uncles in 1954. I remember her funeral and walking from her house to St Patrick's Church the night before. So many people lined the streets. One of my aunts died later that year, and much grief was expressed within the family. I don't remember crying much in those days, and perhaps it was then that I learned to suppress the unhappiness.

Secondary school was interesting, and there were many great teachers there. I had a natural aptitude for mathematics and chemistry. My ambition was to study at Glasgow University, and I achieved this goal in autumn of 1984. Glasgow University changed my life. It was a historical campus with many beautiful buildings. I loved university life. I commuted every day from my hometown, as I didn't live far enough away from the campus to be allowed to stay there. In my penultimate year, I studied psychology for one year, and I wished I had taken the subject in the first year of my studies. I graduated in July 1988 with a Bachelor of Science in Mathematics.

When I studied at Glasgow University, I believed I would never look back. I was a fairly sociable person, and I had no problems meeting new friends. In those days, it was still possible to receive a small grant, initially to cover books, travelling expenses and the contribution to my parents for household expenses. Although I had many friends there, I still tended to socialise with my school friends in Coatbridge. Occasionally we would go to concerts at Glasgow or Strathclyde University. I maintained contact with my school friend Maria for many years and some of the girls who had also gone to university with me from school.

It was difficult in those days to find graduate jobs, and I considered going to college for another year to become a mathematics teacher. However, I became interested in studying for a diploma in accountancy, and I moved to the Riccarton Campus of Heriot-Watt University in Edinburgh for one year.

Living in Edinburgh was a great experience. The campus was about six miles from the City Centre. Whenever we went into the city, I greatly admired the castle and the old town. Students from all over the world attended the university, but mainly from Norway, Ireland and England. I enjoyed the course, although it was demanding. I stayed in the halls of residence and shared with Aina, a Norwegian girl; Helene, a French girl; and Agatha from Tanzania. Also in the same corridor was Arvid from Munich and three other English guys. My friends, Greig and Ahsan from my course, also lived in the halls of residence. We had a great time on campus. Every night, we would have dinner together and discuss our day. I became interested in foreign music, and I introduced them to the music I liked too. In fact, in those early days at Heriot-Watt, I felt like the foreigner in my own country! It was difficult to make myself understood at times. I also became interested in travelling that year, and I planned to visit my friends in their respective countries. I kept in touch with them by writing or phoning, and I did visit Aina in Oslo on several occasions and Arvid in Munich throughout the years. With email and the Internet, it became easier to keep in touch in the following years. Their lives had changed too, which sometimes made visiting them more difficult.

I was very fortunate when I left Heriot-Watt University in 1990 to find a traineeship as a chartered accountant in my hometown of Coatbridge. It was difficult to settle, however, as the last year had been very interesting with international friends; also, working in my own town presented certain challenges. The staff were supportive, though, and I learned a great deal in the four years I worked there. There was block release for the courses, and I passed the final exam first try. After qualifying as a chartered accountant in 1994, it was time to move on, as I had always wanted to work in Glasgow.

Trying to find work in Glasgow in 1994 was difficult. I registered with employment agencies, and they all said the same thing: it was difficult to move to larger firms after training in a small one. I persevered though, and I mainly found contract work for the next two years. It was well paid, and I still managed to go on holidays, but there was no job security. I had to join new firms, learn to deal with different ways of working, new clients and different computer systems, so it was quite stressful, not knowing whether there would be another contract. I was constantly looking for permanent work.

In 1996, I found permanent work in a firm of chartered accountants, and it was the happiest I had been since my training contract had finished. In the early days, I thought I had a good opportunity there. When I was interviewed for the job, I liked the partner, and I thought I would remain there for most of my career. The work was interesting, and I was out of the office, working at client premises most of the time. At times, it was difficult, as there was not a great support system should anything go wrong.

After a few years, I did feel pressured with the work and the environment. I started worrying about meeting the never-ending deadlines, coping with the clients and ultimately keeping my job. It led to sleepless nights, and by 1999, I was becoming ill emotionally. I suppose there were signs, but I was unaware of them. I was stressed all the time, and I found it difficult to switch off from thinking about my problems. The work was on my mind twenty-four hours a day. Even when I was out socially, I was thinking about what I had to do the next day. One of my colleagues was a great help to me, and he tried to assist me at times, but unfortunately, I became ill because of a nervous breakdown in January 1999.

There were other reasons why I had been stressed. I was worried about my dad, as he had to undergo heart bypass surgery within the next year, and we were unaware how successful these operations were at the time. My dad had to retire from work at this time and wait for the operation to take place. Therefore, there were high demands being placed on me with respect to work and my personal life.

Different people have various methods for coping with pressure. There are many thresholds for stress, depending on the activity required and the person involved. Nowadays, health professionals suggest that we walk in nature in order to release stress. I find walking with purpose is helpful.

Whatever the reason for the breakdown in my health, it was the first time I realised the social stigma of having the illness and the problems associated with trying to return to work. Losing work is not only a financial problem, but there is also the loss of identity related to one's profession. I was known for being a chartered accountant, and for several years, I drifted, trying to find alternative purpose to my life.

CHAPTER

Mary's Prayer

M y faith has always been important to me. It has carried me through many difficult years. From an early age, music was also essential to my life. I listened to it at school, at home and at church. It was predominantly the music of John Lennon and the Beatles that I listened to during my confinement, but I love all kinds of music. Searching for answers to why I had suffered a nervous breakdown and subsequent relapses led me to study for a degree in psychology. Education had been important in the lives of our family. Travel has been instrumental in changing my life, through learning about different cultures. However, in the years when I was ill and unable to leave my own country, I became reacquainted with the beauty of Scotland and the strength of our people. It is interesting that although we travel, we still retain our own identity. Meeting people from different countries allows us to see that there are other ways of life. Once I had recovered significantly, I travelled to Liverpool, England, which re-energised me and afforded me a new direction.

"Mary's Prayer" was a number-one hit by the Scottish band Danny Wilson in 1988 (Clark 1987). The band members were Gary and Kit Clark and Ged Grimes, now of Simple Minds. The year it was a hit in the charts was very important in my life because I graduated from Glasgow University. I knew I wanted to write the story of how I recovered from a long-term illness and managed to turn my life around. In September 2012, I contacted Gary Clark, who wrote the song and I am very happy to say that he gave me his blessing to use the title for my book.

This song was always special to me, and it had greater significance as I grew older.

In times of despair, I prayed relentlessly, asking for help and often feeling that my pleas would remain unanswered prayers. It was at Lourdes in France that I first realised the power of prayer. There, people from all over the world come to the Grotto at Massabielle, where the Virgin Mary was thought to appear to St. Bernadette, to pray for their loved ones. I believe that great gifts were bestowed on me that day, and I may have even experienced a miracle. In Lourdes, I felt humbled by the people who carried their cross with a feeling of acceptance. It was during that pilgrimage that I really experienced the presence of God and the strength of the human spirit.

The reason I chose this song title for the book is that it is my prayer for society and in particular people affected by mental illness who are marginalised by society, so that they may find peace in the twenty-first century. In the past, people suffering from such illnesses were locked in institutions, disabled by brain surgery or by medications. I hope that this would encourage future research of a phenomenological nature into the subject and shed some light on the uniqueness of the human experience. (Phenomenology is the study of the lived experience of an individual.)

My life was turned upside down by a depressive illness, which I attribute mainly to the high-pressure environment in which I worked at the time and the lack of understanding I received when I returned to work. I had followed the rule book, making sure I had a good education and a profession, yet illness is a great equalizer. It was a lonely place to be and a difficult situation to cope with because even my family did not really understand why I was in this circumstance, and I did not discuss it with my friends.

Somehow, in the last few years, I managed to meet the right people, and I was drawn to the right books, films, songs, and singers that provided insights for me. Unfortunately, being on benefits with debts to pay, I was not in a position to travel to India to find myself like the protagonist did in *Eat, Pray, Love*. Therefore, I had to find myself in my own hometown, in Glasgow and in the city of Liverpool. Actually, I found myself in books and in the lyrics of songs. In spending more time with my family, I found common bonds which would have not have been identified had I not been ill. Studying for a degree in psychology has been an amazing journey. I have grown and also found some solutions for my own problems, which I hope will help others move forward in their lives. I decided to take this route because I had the time to study for the course and I wanted to prove to myself that I could still perform well in exams.

Maybe *Mary's Prayer* will make people realise that they should exercise their civil rights and ask for better treatment or second opinions. It would be a step forward if the cycle of return periods in the hospitals were broken and they had a more relaxed atmosphere. My hope is that this book will raise awareness to eradicate the stigma.

The "See Me" mental-health campaign in Scotland has been successful over the last decade or so. It asks that people who are not ill actually see the sufferers as people and not as the label they were diagnosed with. Ironically, at the time I'm writing this chapter, someone I had known throughout this period made me realise that he did not "see me" either – despite my achievements prior to and after the breakdown. For a few days, this fact caused me some pain; however, I quickly moved on and realised that the person involved was not the character I had believed him to be. It made me reflect; that if a person as qualified as myself, felt less because of these superficial comments, then how would someone feel who had not worked for many years because of their illness. Such a person would probably feel that confiding in someone was worthless because they lacked understanding of the illness and the sufferer's unique story. I asked everyone imaginable for help but to no avail. I still found it impossible to return to the workforce.

Reflections on this fourteen-year period of illness are easier now because I am far enough removed from it to feel somewhat detached from the experience. I hope that in years to come, I feel the same way. I believe that the way of thinking I had then perhaps contributed to the breakdown of my health. I hope that in future, there would be an extreme unlikelihood of this ever happening again.

Whilst going in search of answers, you sometimes find more than you were actually looking for. I found many truths about myself which I was forced to confront, and I kept the faith throughout this experience.

It was my introduction to humanistic psychology that helped me come to terms with the fact that perhaps I did not have to delve into the distant past to solve my recurring problems. I knew that to go where I wanted to required only a subtle change in my way of thinking; it would be necessary to take action towards these goals. However, it was reflections on my childhood that made me revisit the past. Unlike in psychoanalysis, humanistic psychology does not look for answers in the past, but rather concentrates on how the patient can move forward. It is therefore possible to transcend your experiences.

The period of confinement during which I had little contact with people my own age seemed rather harsh. In this way, I no longer feel I have to ask "Why me?" but to say "There by the grace of God", I was healed by the power of prayer. I hope my story will lighten the hearts of those who suffer in silence in the community or within their own walls.

Music was a major influence throughout my life. Most of my family had to have a song to sing at family parties. I have a vast repertoire of songs, and I remember most of the lyrics too. As a young child, I loved Elvis Presley, John Lennon, the Beatles, and Kate Bush. Then, as a teenager, I moved on to listening to Madonna and Sting, whom I still love. Music has always been the backdrop to my life. In many ways, listening to music was a very healing experience, and I drew great strength from the lyrics of the songs.

Some of the most important information I have ever learned in my life was from the New Thought Movement. This movement focused on having good thoughts or vibrations. The theory behind it is based on the Law of Attraction, whereby "like attracts like". We are thought to attract whatever we want into our lives through higher vibrational states, the highest vibrational state being that of love. Therefore, concentrating on feelings of love or images of what you enjoy doing will increase your vibrational states. The New Thought Movement was also concerned with healing through thought control. It has changed my life, and I hope the emphasis on these methods in this book will change people's lives. The method of thought control is exceptionally good for people with mood disorders, as you learn how to alter your mood by listening to music, etc. We live our lives without knowing exactly where we came from. Genealogy, which has become increasingly important to many people these days, can take you back several generations.

Synchronicity has been important to me throughout my life, although I do not think I was consciously aware of this until the last five years. Somehow, the right people appeared in my life like magic, and they moved me forward in the most amazing way. Belief in Christianity defines me, and I am grateful that my parents brought me up in the Catholic faith. My belief in the Virgin Mary is absolute, and there is no doubt in my mind that in the small hours of the morning, when I cannot sleep, she is there. Also, I know that sometimes I have wanted something that was not perfect for me, and it was disallowed, like in the Garth Brooks song, "Unanswered Prayers" (Brooks 1990). In this song, he thanks God for unanswered prayers because otherwise he would not be with his wife.

Education had been my salvation. The Waterboys song, "The Whole of the Moon", reflects on this point, in that sometimes it is the people who don't travel but read about a place who actually see more than the voyager (Scott 1985). The meaning of *life* or *success* means different things to different people. The uniqueness of the desires of a person should be celebrated. Our life should be rich and abundant, not just with money but with human experience. Phenomenology studies this and concentrates on temporality, spatiality, embodiment, and power relations. Temporality concentrates on the concept of time, which in my life seemed to have changed speed throughout the fourteen years from 1999 until 2013. At times it was too fast and at other times much too slow. When I was working in Glasgow, my life had been very fast; between work and my social life, I hardly had time to think or contemplate what I wanted to do next. I suppose I thought I was happy and I was doing what I wanted to do at the time, but I did feel insecure about my future. I was taking Spanish classes in the evenings, which was a good way to meet people. I loved the language, and it was great to meet people outside my working life. The contrast when I stopped working was like night and day. I often wondered how I could fill the days. Time moved very slowly, and it was difficult to adapt to the changes in my life. The concept of spatiality suggests that someone may feel distant emotionally even when there is not geographical distance. I experienced distance physically and mentally from people during the period when I was ill. I felt as though I was at a great emotional distance from my friends and colleagues, whose lives continued whilst mine stopped abruptly. It seemed as though they did not really understand my new life, and they found it difficult to relate to me. There was distance too, as many friendships ended because I couldn't meet the people because of my financial situation. Embodiment was important because I gained weight because of the medications for the illness, which increased my appetite too. This concept explains how we relate to the world through our bodies. I felt heavy and slowed up because of the extra weight gain.

Phenomenological psychology originates from philosophical roots by Edmund Husserl (1859–1938), and it uses qualitative methods to interpret data. This type of research places the importance on the reflections of the interviewee, and it is important for the researcher to approach the topic as though he has no knowledge of it, which is known as bracketing or Epoché. In order to carry out this research, he must accept the lived experience of the individual without judgement. Although this experience is unique to people, we have a shared understanding about every subject in the universe. Therefore, the phenomenological research is very similar to existential theory, which is the concept of being. Its association with existence therefore reflects on the uniqueness, action taking place, freedom of choice, and the place where they live at that time in the world. This type of research is carried out by the use of interviews, which are then interpreted for emergent themes.

I am grateful that I live in this time and that with medication, I have recovered well from the breakdowns. Perhaps in an earlier period, I would not have been as fortunate.

During our time on Earth, we have much work to do to educate ourselves, love our family and friends, and enjoy life. In many ways, despite the challenges I have met in my life, I can honestly say that in some ways, I have been lucky. I have travelled, received a great education, worked hard, and found love. I can honestly say that I find more to like than to dislike in the world. However, change is necessary in order to grow, and we need to eradicate the cognitive rigidity that exists in the hearts and souls of many people.

Destiny brought us here to this point in our lives, in the centre of the universe; perhaps tomorrow it will lead us somewhere we would never have expected to go. If anything, the search for answers here and in the last fourteen years made me realise who I am and why I am here.

CHAPTER

Finding Peace in the Twenty-First Century

In the past fourteen years, I have searched for the answers in every self-help book I could find. I thought the gurus or the writers of these books could shine a light on the truth of why I had lost most of my thirties to the darkest period of my life. In conclusion, I found my way through the tunnel, gradually receiving more light, until my eyes adjusted to this new level of awareness. Evidently, it is essential not to receive too much light too soon, or we could lose our sight. Peace is often found at the point of acceptance, when we decide things must change and take action towards that goal. Sometimes we have to go with the flow to see what happens, but we must walk towards our goals; otherwise our circumstances will not change.

Yesterday, I met with my former high school English teacher, Benny Timpson, to discuss what he had reviewed in my writings. I felt a degree of apprehension, as in some ways,

I could imagine myself as the sixteen-year-old, handing in an essay to be marked.

Someone once said that when the student is ready, the teacher will appear. I believe this has been the case in my life. Call it divine inspiration or whatever you will, I contacted him because I believed him to be a great English teacher. He was knowledgeable in his subject and had extensive knowledge of social matters. I did not know at this time that he had also studied sociology in his degree. Finding someone with a social conscience can be difficult these days, and also the qualitative work in social psychology I prefer is English-based; therefore, it was essential to seek a mentor who could provide this depth of reflection.

By a strange coincidence, the school in which my sister taught merged with my old high school. Therefore, for a few years, Lena was working with Benny Timpson. I met him at the funeral of a friend of mine, and then it was in the process of writing the book that I contacted him. At that time, I had an idea for writing a book, but it took many years to materialise.

Many success books in America promote the idea of having a mentor. There are various Mastermind groups that suggest you should learn from books written by the most successful people in your field. I started studying the books of these success coaches, and I realised that abundance was not just about having financial success but also personal happiness. This was actually the start of my recovery period, as I could see doors of opportunity opening, rather than seeing the obstacles that were there before.

In many ways, I felt childlike after these breakdowns, having to relearn to focus on reading. I had tremendous curiosity when studying the child-development module of the psychology degree, as I could apply it to the way I was relearning to experience the world.

With respect to the development of the child, there are two important psychological perspectives, those of Jean Piaget (1896–1980) and Lev Vygotsky (1896–1934). Piaget argued that individuals develop more sophisticated mental representations in the environment, and therefore development is their own construction Furthermore, he proposed that the child could learn alone and in many ways has the curiosity of a scientist, discovering the world, whereas the Vygotskian approach alternatively states that the teacher is required to direct children in pursuit of further knowledge. The information is therefore supplied when the child is prepared for it, and through the process of scaffolding, is supported until the child understands the concepts completely. Scaffolding therefore as a construction is removed when the child is confident enough to support him- or herself (Oates, Sheehy and Wood 2005). My understanding of this is that the more gifted child will have less need for the teacher; however, teachers can direct these children in a way that will open the door of opportunity for them. As an adult, I believe that it is advantageous to have a mentor or teacher, even if this person only recommends a book to read or a film to watch. So it was that I found myself in a very profound discussion with the teacher who inspired me all those years ago. We had both faced trials with our health and had experienced what it was like to be on the receiving end of others' limited views of our future capacity.

For the most part, I was learning alone in a Piagetian way, like the scientist discovering new things. The Internet was a great learning experience, and I read widely.

Social construction theory states that people construct meaning through language used between at least two people. In many ways, then, the communication we have with another person helps to facilitate greater understanding of a specific dilemma. Language has always been important to me, whether it has been the written word in a book or in the lyrics of a song. The construction of meaning acts as a key between people, which helps us walk forward to a new understanding. A person can also change his or her opinions in this way, through reading a book or watching a movie because there is dialogue. I felt I was changing because of what I was reading; a lot of the stagnant thought patterns were being replaced by the ideology I had learned from the books I was reading. Words tend to resonate with us, and we may have a favourite quotation which we feel actually defines us. The search for meaning has taken me on the most wonderful voyage of self-discovery.

My journey through the contours of my mind took me to many places, through rivers, over mountains, and helped me resolve matters by building bridges. Evidently, I did want to move forward in my life and to build bridges to metaphorically move to the other side, away from my problems. No doubt, in those early days, I did contemplate the "why me?" thoughts, but I now understand that this period of suffering was essential for my personal growth and salvation.

So it is I find myself changed, no longer the person who believes that all people are good but who makes decisions on the goodness of people when I meet them, not judging them by their race, religion, or profession. For the people I do not know, I cannot judge their lives; that is for God to decide at the end of days. In some ways, I miss my younger self, in that

I had great enthusiasm for life, and I believed then that one person could change the world. In some ways, I still think this is possible with the right person involved. From this moment on, I accept the words of St Francis of Assisi, that there are things we cannot change.

Malcesine, Italy and Lourdes, France

M alcesine—the name invokes so many memories. In the darkest days that followed, somehow the light still shone there, beckoning me back to a time when my life was more glamorous and affluent.

Malcesine is a town in Lake Garda, in the north of Italy. For several summers in the 1990s, I found some comfort there, through the most difficult period of my life. I was unhappy in my work and personal life. My sister, Lena, and I still booked the two-week package holiday with Thomson's in those days. We looked forward to our time there, and somehow, even the difficult experiences at work could be transcended until we reached our beloved destination. It was different days, as we used to plan the holiday in detail before we went there. We knew many of the locals because we visited the area often and we took day trips to Venice, Verona, and Padua.

In January 1999, I experienced a traumatic breakdown. There is seemingly no one reason for a breakdown, and it can take many years to come to this point. However, at the time, my father was due to have heart-bypass surgery, and I was unhappy with the pressure at work. I recovered within three months with medication, and I returned to work.

Thoughts of Malcesine remained with me during that fourteen-year period from 1999 until 2013, when I had been intermittently ill. Malcesine still represents to me a time when there were endless possibilities and opportunities in my life. In fact, when I had trouble sleeping, my mother always instructed me to close my eyes and imagine that I was in Malcesine. Sleeping at night in those days was a problem. So I travelled to Malcesine in my mind every night. I could visualise the Scaligeri Castle, the cobblestones of the old town, and the beautiful lake. Also, I recognised my old self there, wearing the vibrant colours in my dress, and I remembered the great expectations I had for my life at that time.

Life changed dramatically for me in the year 2000. I suffered a relapse after being taken off medication. The symptoms were the same as during the breakdown. I was initially taken off medication on a trial basis, but unfortunately I relapsed after six months. It was nine months this time before I returned to work. I was dissuaded from returning there by my health professionals, my employer, and my family, just in case I had another relapse. I was unable to obtain permanent employment again in my own field of accountancy, so it may or may not have made a difference to my career. However, at the time, I believed it was the correct decision, and my employer allowed me to return to work. Soon afterwards, the standard of my work was questioned, and it resulted in disciplinary action against me. I remembered at the time thinking that this nightmare would end soon, but unfortunately, thirteen years later, I still have not had permanent employment.

Looking back now, I received no support whatsoever, even though my employer was aware that I had experienced a traumatic breakdown. I felt the staff distanced themselves, and I also retreated inside myself, feeling ashamed about my illness and the changes in my appearance. Social psychology taught me that the adaptation to these changes was challenging. As embodiment issues increased, my self-esteem decreased. Embodiment is how we relate to the world through our bodies. People had always spoken to me about feeling alone in a crowded room, and it was only then I truly experienced it.

I remember that another member of staff had been ill when I returned to work, and I was asked to contribute money to buy flowers. I was told that she was really ill and she deserved the flowers. It was then that I fully understood the impact of the invisible illness; because of lack of knowledge, people did not appreciate the extent of the illness, nor did they want to offer any support. Likewise, I did not want to talk too much about it, as I did not expect much empathy. There were many remarks – too numerous to recount – which made me feel undervalued. Perhaps the stigma of mental-health problems at that time was too great to have even one person cross the barrier, saying some words of comfort or even just that they understood.

Somehow, life continued after I left this office in April 2004. My family were supportive about this decision; however, we were not particularly affluent. I did not know the way forward, and unfortunately for me, no one else seemed to appreciate the challenges I would face in the years to come. The doctors were supportive too, with respect to writing letters. They were genuinely concerned, but there was very little after-care support in those days. The medication I had been given had nasty side effects, like excessive weight gain and extreme tiredness. I would sleep for at least two hours every afternoon. I did not fit into any of my clothes, and it was expensive to replace them. I felt very unattractive in the only clothes I could buy, which were old-fashioned. I had nightmares that I could not share with anyone about my experiences, both at work and in the hospital. I felt like I was experiencing the same sentiments which were expressed in the U2 song, "Stuck in a Moment". I was trapped and I could not move on from the moment.

In July 2004, my family generously took me to Lourdes in France for one week. There had been reported apparitions there of the Virgin Mary, who appeared to Bernadette Soubirious some 150 years earlier. It is a world-famous pilgrimage site where people travel from all over the world to find peace and solace in their time of need. Many come to Lourdes looking for a miracle from Our Lady of Lourdes, and I believe most of them find what they are looking for in the Grotto of Massabielle. My family had absolute faith in Our Lady of Lourdes, and we were looking for help to change my circumstances. I did not ask her for a miracle, only that I should find direction and that the obstacles around me should be removed. I believe she has now granted me this wish.

In Lourdes, I found peace and comfort, knowing there were people who were more deserving of cures from Our Lady than

I. In many ways, that experience changed my life. Sometimes we don't see the changes in our lives until we reflect on earlier years. These critical incidents assist the evolution of our spirits. At Lourdes, I was mesmerised by the daily processions and the people who came to bathe in the holy waters. I am now convinced I experienced a miracle at Lourdes, because when I returned to Scotland, I met some people who changed the course of my life. I was granted the direction, and I was shown the way.

It is difficult to explain what changed in me when I visited Lourdes. Prior to this period, I couldn't see the way forward. Although I had returned to work after the illness, I felt that every piece of work I completed was scrutinised very closely. Trying to meet my deadlines was difficult too. I lost confidence in my ability. I was very tired with the medication, and I was returning home after work to sleep for a few hours. As soon as I arrived in Lourdes, I felt much different. There was an excitement about the place and hopeful looks on everyone's faces – even those of the very ill. I felt relaxed for the first time in years, and somehow I felt things could change.

I can still map out the town in my mind; there was something quite magical the first time I waited in the procession to approach the grotto. Many people in front of me touched the walls of the grotto as they waited to reach the Statue of Our Lady, all the while relentlessly praying for their special requests. I had seen pictures of it, but nothing could prepare me for the feeling of peace and release I experienced there. To have peace of mind must be a wonderful place to be. To a certain degree, I have attained it, but not in the absolute, because I have not been able to move forward financially.

I loved the pilgrimage my family and I made to Lourdes in 2004. We did not visit as part of a church group, preferring to make our own private pilgrimage. I have absolute faith in the Virgin Mary. Frequently at night, my sister and I would visit the grotto and pray quietly for our personal intentions. I believe my prayers were answered, as I felt greatly motivated to effect change in my life.

When I returned to Scotland, I was referred by my GP to see a new psychiatrist, who changed my life. She was young and extremely interested in my case, and for the first time in many years, I felt hopeful that her influence could alter the next few years of my life. Within a few weeks, she had reduced the medication and greatly improved the quality of my life. I will always be entirely grateful for her intervention and for listening closely to the work-related stress that had led to my ill health. She had tremendous insight into the situations people find themselves in at work. However, in those days I had lost a lot of confidence, and I never fully discussed the extent of the problems I had suffered at work.

Reflecting on these days now still fills me with a sense of anxiety. It has taken me many years and studying for a degree in psychology to even manage to see the tip of the iceberg. The last breakdown was more of a breakthrough, where I researched the cause of the repeated relapses and I changed my methods for dealing with people and problems. Nowadays, I survive on a low maintenance dose, and I achieve most of what I did prior to the illness.

In the last three years, I have been studying for a degree in psychology with the Open University. I have searched for answers for my ill health, researched many case studies and publications, and looked for remedies of a permanent nature. I found *The Journey* by Brandon Bays and *The Sedona Method* by Hale Dwoskin. I believe that the solution lies within oneself, and in the words of John Lennon, "I found that the Lord helps those who help themselves" (Lennon, Double Fantasy 2000). I considered asking permission to use the title of this song "Help Me to Help Myself" for the title of this book. The humanistic perspective does not look for answers in the past but rather leads us forward from where we are today to the place we want to go to in the future. It is holistic in nature and focuses on the environment and the situation which one finds oneself, a situation that could be changed by taking action towards one's goals. I believe it is difficult for the families of people who become ill in this way because of the length of time it takes to recover.

Last year, I returned to Malcesine. Lena and I walked the routes I had visualised in my mind. After the financial ruin I found myself in because of the final breakdown, it was a miracle in itself that I stood there by the lake. The first time I visited the area, I was convinced of the presence of God. I was in awe of the tremendous beauty of the lakes and mountains there. I thought if heaven looked like this, I would not mind travelling there. So I thank my mother for her assistance in making me transcend my circumstances through my visits through dreams to Malcesine. Without the support of my family, my GP, and my consultant, it is unlikely that I would be here to tell this story. So I thank them and also John Lennon, whose music has helped me through the darkness and who has inspired me for most of my life. So it is with the grace of God go I, and with his help, I will try now to campaign for change.

Hopefully, people who read this book will see that sometimes it is when you are against all odds that the strength of character is revealed. Change is necessary in our world. Somehow, people who don't fit the norm can sometimes find themselves on the inside looking out, rather than the outside looking in. Try to "see me" in the pages of this book, and hopefully in seeing me, you will see others who have travelled a similar road and find understanding for those who are lost to us.

As a teenager in high school, studying modern studies, I was a great believer in civil and human rights. In those days, as my friend Gerry used to say, I was a politician, always saying the right thing. Always agreeable and being all things to all people. My hero, then and even now, is St Thomas More, who died for his beliefs. So, in the same vein, I will tell you my story, and perhaps you will think I could have taken an alternative route.

CHAPTER

The Whole of the Moon

I believe that today I understood the significance of The
Waterboys song regarding seeing the "whole of the moon"
(Scott 1985). I loved this song many years ago, and it still
has great meaning for me after all this time. It has taken me
fourteen years to find the right path that would take me to the
place where I wanted to go. There are twelve astrological signs
in the zodiac, and the number is significant to moving into a
new phase. Somehow, I felt that if that fourteen-year period
passed, perhaps my life would improve. On Saturday, I had a
day school at Stirling University for the Open University course
in social psychology. There is a lake there, and while I waited to
be collected by my family, I walked around it. Many memories of
university life flooded back to me, and I was filled with a feeling
of complete joy and contentment. I thought of the Yoko Ono
song, "Hard Times" (Ono, Double Fantasy 1980), in which she
had a moment when she appreciated that the difficult times
had passed.

The Waterboys's song "The Whole of the Moon" is the story of one person who travelled the world and saw the crescent of the moon, whilst another person just stayed in his room and through books, etc., managed to see the whole of the moon (Scott 1985). I believe that it is true in life, that often, the closer we inspect a place, the more we fail to stand back to see the bigger picture. This relates to my own experience because during this fourteen-year period I did not travel much through Europe, but I read widely about places I would like to visit and learned a great deal from my psychology course. I stayed at home most of the time and listened to music or read books.

Three years ago, I found the Sedona Method. The *Sedona Method* was developed by Lester Levenson, who was an engineer and was told that he would die in his forties after a heart attack. He walked for seven hours and started to feel better, and he designed a programme of emotional release. He lived for another forty years after this experience. The Sedona Method facilitates change in people by allowing them to focus on their problems and then release them. My friend, Lilia Sinclair introduced me to the technique, which is very powerful and much quicker than learning to meditate. I believe it to be more effective than other methods, and it has longer-lasting effects.

I first heard it mentioned in the film *The Secret*. Many people were sceptical about this film, but it was impossible to ignore this new way of thinking. In fact, it was not very new, as it was based on a book by Wallace D Wattles called *The Science of Getting Rich,* which was written over one hundred years ago. It was this book and the research I did into the New Thought

Movement that finally helped me to find peace. The practices in the books relate to the Bible and thoughts from the beginning of early civilisation, which allowed people to be abundant in their lives.

CHAPTER

Let It Be

The last fourteen years of my life have been very different from what I imagined they would be. As an ambitious chartered accountant, I expected to have made it to partner and to have been very affluent by this time, had everything gone to plan. Somehow, the story of my life changed by force, and I had to follow a different path.

In the early years after my illness, I did feel guilty about not working, and I was always trying to talk myself into returning to work. When I did return, I had actually lost all my self-confidence. I am not sure about how much the staff were informed about my condition.

I periodically had to visit the consultant at the hospital and my own GP. The early days at the hospital were not good, as the juniors had to scribe for the consultant. My mother usually attended these meetings with me, and we were instructed when to speak and when not to speak. In the consultant, I found someone who did not listen to the problems I had experienced in the workplace; I also had problems expressing myself at the time.

I had lost confidence in my ability to perform the most basic of activities. This was because of the breakdowns and the anxiety I experienced following them. I often thought about travelling to work on the train, and I did experience social anxiety about it. This was strange, thinking back, as I had travelled on the trains into Glasgow since I was 18 years of age, studying at Glasgow University. I remember the hospital meetings with at least eight people in attendance to hear my case. I still believe that this is unjust for a person who is trying to return to health. I felt self-conscious talking about my problems in front of so many people, and it did impede my recovery.

There I met many people from all walks of life, who had all succumbed to illness for many different reasons. It was a mixed ward, although men and women were in different rooms. It was not an ideal situation for people in a vulnerable state. My mother used to worry about my safety and suggested to the nursing staff that this setup should be changed. Initially, I was in a separate room, and I am not sure how much the staff could watch every room through the night. Some people did not want to be discharged, which I couldn't understand at the time, but now I understand that the community may be a more frightening place for them. It was not a pleasant experience, and the discipline was draconian. The staff started holding hope meetings in the mornings and recovery meetings at night. Some educational card games were used that incorporated moral issues. There was very little to do in terms of activities, and to be honest, the medication made the patients very drowsy throughout the day. Sometimes I pretended to sleep, especially as some of the patients tended to play DVDs into the night.

I had only been in the hospital for a few weeks to stabilise the condition, but it was a year before I started reading again. In that time, I just listened to music. Somehow, this time I believed the time would pass and I would be able to concentrate again. I struggled dealing with the mail too. The hospital did not offer a great deal of help. I think I would have benefitted from counselling at that time, but none was offered. When people were talking, it was difficult to process what was being said, so joining in the conversation was quite difficult because of the slowing down of the brain.

Whenever I had to go shopping after I had returned home, I was constantly asked why I wasn't working. It was very difficult to admit that I wasn't working because of illness, as there would have been more questions. Looking back, I suppose it may have been easier to make up some physical illness or to have told the truth, but that's not the way it seemed then. My life had been centred professionally and socially in Glasgow. I missed the routine of the work but not the deadlines. In the last two places I had worked on contracts, I was deluged with work.

Soon after, I volunteered to work for an international charity two days per week, which was good because I met some people to talk to. I met a friend there who has helped me over the last few years by meeting to go to the cinema and other places. After four months, however, I felt I would have to find fulfilling work to do, and a few months later, I decided to study psychology with the Open University. This was an amazing benefit, as I did not have to pay for these courses because I was not working, and I started to feel lighter and more invigorated by the learning. As always, education was my salvation.

For the first year after I was ill, I was visited by a community nurse. Most of the time when she visited, I was fairly positive about the future; however, in reality, I did not know the way forward. I visited MPs, lawyers, and many other people for advice during this period, but to no avail. No one seemed to have any suitable answers. I needed advice about how to return to work when I had gaps in my curriculum vitae because of illness. My previous firm had merged with another firm, and it was difficult to obtain a reference. This was, therefore, an impediment to my returning to work.

Because I had just bought a car on hire purchase and had various debts to pay, my family had to help me through this period. In fact, the situation has not moved on yet. I had no social life whatsoever. Some of my friends I had known from my university days fell by the wayside. I no longer feel sad about the loss of these friendships, but at the time I felt quite alone and sad. They had been in my life for twenty years. Maybe we would have grown apart anyway, irrespective of whether I had become ill. I do understand that I wasn't much fun at the time; I was overweight and couldn't keep up with the plans they had because of the money involved. It has been a humbling experience, and sadly, I did find out who my friends were. Strangely enough, on the few occasions we did meet, they made me feel quite low about the age of my car, the fact that I still lived with my parents, or that I wasn't seeing anyone. I would have liked to have lived elsewhere at that time, but realistically I would not have coped on my own during that period. Without my family, I would have been destitute.

Many people ask me why I am not married or why I still live with my parents, and I have to say it bothers me less now than it once did. I would have to admit that my greatest regret is that the illness during my thirties and forties has deprived me of marrying and having a family. I also realise that this had an effect on the lives of my sister and my parents. I suppose I will not have children now, but perhaps this book will help some young people deal with their problems before some crisis intervention takes place and they end up in the vicious circle that I did. I required crisis intervention on the three occasions that I became ill. It is the nature of the illness that you are unaware of how ill you really are, and it is your family who notice changes in your personality or habits.

There have been few people over the years I could confide in about the problems regarding the depressive illness. My family and my doctor did listen, but I am not sure you can fully understand the situation unless you have been there. However, I do thank God, every day for the people who cared, even if they did not fully comprehend what had happened to me. It is difficult to raise the topic of mental illness. I suppose my logic was that if I mentioned it, people would never accept what I said again, and it would become common knowledge throughout the town. If I *didn't* mention it, they may conclude that I was just unemployed and that I could not be that great an accountant.

There was a tremendous loss of identity during that fourteen-year period from 1999 until 2013, when I was unable to find permanent work. I stayed at home most of the time and avoided the extended-family reunions. Several relatives died during these years, and although I attended these funerals, I felt very awkward and avoided talking about my life. My sister and I couldn't really travel through this period, which people must have found unusual. I did miss it, but I was so depressed most of the time that I didn't really notice the vacations much at all. I suffered from a depressive illness, which was the reason for the hospitalisation. The obstacles seemed so great that no matter who I asked for advice, no one had a workable solution. So I lost myself in music, mainly by John Lennon and the Beatles.

My healthcare professionals were not very positive about the future. Most of them advised me to change to a less-stressful career and to lower the goalposts. It wasn't until I recently studied psychology that I understood that people assess you in relation to themselves and their abilities. Most of them were not in a position to judge the career of a chartered accountant, with respect to what type of work was involved on a daily basis.

My favourite field in psychology is that of individual differences, and in particular, Personal Construct Theory by George Kelly. The uniqueness of life experience, phenomenologically, is extremely difficult to critique, and it would require extensive research, but I do believe that the answer to the mental health problems of individuals lies there. Whilst reflecting in the interviews in a phenomenological perspective, although the experience may be unique to an individual, when cross-checking other interviews of participants, it is striking how much common ground there is, when at the end, we all want to be loved, to have fulfilling work, and to have a nice house and some enjoyment with friends and family. The uniqueness of the human experience must be focused on because many people have different reasons for becoming ill.

Throughout this time, I had to develop patience. This has been extremely difficult for me, and I did not consider myself impatient previously in my life. Yoko Ono's song "Season of Glass" has always held significance for me when I think of that time when she reflected on the season that never passed (Ono, Season of Glass 1981). I identified with this song because, like Yoko Ono, I had to deal with being indoors behind the glass. I wasn't really happy with my life, but I was unable and unready to join the world outside. Yes, sadly, I also experienced the "season of glass." I couldn't move on during this time. There was no social life, no love interest in my life, no employment, no money, and not many friends. Without my immediate family and the music, I could not tell you where I may be today. So it was that I lived inside the house, looking out of the window, watching life as an observer without taking part in it at that time.

I believe that the answer to mental illness will be found in qualitative, social psychological research and not in quantitative research.

A friend recommended a book called *The Celestine Prophecy*, an adventure by Stephen Redfield, which is a fictional story set in Peru about the shift in human consciousness predicted to take place at the end of the twentieth century. It talks of synchronicity, which was the life work of Carl Jung, stating that coincidences would accelerate in people's lives which were actual signs of change from God or the universe. In fact, the book focuses on the point that there are no coincidences. Since reading the book, I have been more aware of these reflections in my own life. Amazingly, I met the right people at the right time to move me forward in my life. Also, many people returned to my life to help.

CHAPTER

Identity

Perhaps the most important thing in life is to have a sense of collective identity. This means different things to different people. However, it is this sense of belonging to a group that prevents us from feeling isolated and promotes the connectedness that is so important to us throughout our lives.

Identity is often thought of as a type of personality, how we appear to others, our profession or our trade, which often defines us. When asked who we are, a person may say she is a doctor or a teacher, for example. It was interesting to me that when I became ill and lost this sense of professional identity, I began to look at the bigger picture about who I really was and what path I was walking. In the years when I didn't work, I often felt I was no longer the accountant who had travelled all over Scotland on audits and met with numerous clients throughout the day. I did this type of work until I became ill. In some cases, I was working one day, and I would return home feeling quite ill the next day. Sometimes the breakdowns happened overnight. I had three

43

breakdowns in the fourteen-year period from 1999 until 2013. At times I questioned my own intelligence and whether I had indeed suffered some cognitive deterioration after each breakdown. Of course, life continued for me, but my heart wasn't in the meetings I had with friends, and no doubt they saw many changes in me.

I have changed completely since the last period of illness because I no longer feel that I have to please people the way I did previously. If asked now, I would say I had experienced ill health, but I wouldn't labour on it too much.

It is interesting to look at the early development of identity in relation to this discussion because there is a certain degree of relearning required after a person has suffered a breakdown. In my case, I had to learn to read again and regain my confidence in a social setting. I lost the ability to concentrate to read. We all have a sense of who we are, but when this breakdown of my health happened, even if like me the person had been very confident previously, it is difficult to do even the most routine tasks without assistance. Family and friends would constantly tell me I could no longer do the job I had trained for, because of this. No one understands the situation unless they have walked in your shoes, and even then they might not have had to undergo the same experience. I met many doctors, nurses, and friends who could tell me where I went wrong, but they would have struggled too if they had found themselves in my situation. Everyone had an opinion about my life and how I could have taken an alternative route and not ended up in such a competitive environment. I suppose I should have left after the first time I became ill. So my experience has now taught me to listen to my heart and what my own intuition tells me.

CHAPTER

The Garden of the Soul

*T*he *Garden of the Soul* was the title of the prayer book my grandmother gave me before her death in 1974. I have reflected on the title over the years when I became ill, even though I spent little time in the garden. Since studying psychology, it has impacted on me with respect to the nature-versus-nurture debate as to whether it is also genetic or environmental, whilst some people succumb to mental illness and others do not.

From my own experience, it is the environments in which we find ourselves, whether it is where we live or work, which bring about this inability to function or to cope with our everyday situations. The soil in the garden must be watered every day and have the proper conditions in order for the plants to grow strong and flourish. Such is the case with people and their ability to establish a good life.

As Dr Wayne Dyer reflects in his *There Is a Spiritual Solution to Every Problem* DVD, we are spiritual beings having a human

45

experience and not the other way around (Dyer 2007). The soul is infinite and has existed prior to our birth and will exist beyond the grave. It is therefore necessary to concentrate on what it takes to feed the soul and the body.

The soul can be fed through spirituality. This can be achieved in different ways, through prayer, doing good works, and ultimately reaching a state of contentment. Happiness comes from within, and it cannot be relied upon to be experienced through another person.

In the garden of the soul, there are many different types of flowers and plants that need nurturing. We all enjoy being unique and pursuing different interests. It is not for me to say that listening to the music that I did or reading the same books would bring about the same change in your life. However, following this lead could change your life.

The Universal Source, or God, which gives us life each day and allows Creation to take place helps us to grow every day – spiritually, physically, and emotionally. The seasons change; there is a time to live and to die. Destiny moves us forward, and we meet the right people at the right time. Perhaps someone mentions a new book to us which helps to change our opinions.

It is important to spend time in the garden and enjoy the outdoors. Children these days spend more time playing with their computers rather than being outside in nature, which will no doubt impact on their lives in the years to come. Doctors are now advising patients to read self-help books or to take up walking and gentle exercise outdoors, rather than run on the treadmill at the gym. Walking with purpose can change your life. We find in the garden that there are other life forms we may not like, but they are necessary for the creation of something very beautiful, like the bees. We all have our place in the cycle of life.

PART II

Universal Problems

CHAPTER

Against All Odds

It is important at this stage to consider the impact the fourteen-year period of illness and eventual recovery had on my family as well as myself. The first period of illness in 1999 lasted for three months. The second breakdown happened in 2000, after being taken off medication, and the last relapse took place in 2008, again after being taken off medication. When my father retired from work because of ill health, it was my sister who became the breadwinner. I can see the effect this has had on her life, as she struggled to work and gave up the expensive holidays to Italy to save me from bankruptcy. I believe that she placed duty and responsibility before her own needs. If she ever confided in anyone about the nature of my illness, I am unaware of it. As we matured in age through this period, there were also many jibes about why we were not in relationships and were going on breaks together.

So it was that my family found ourselves in a situation with which we had no experience and found little help from the outside world to deal with it. I assume because I had experienced years of good health in between, the last one did come as a shock.

Looking back on this point, I wonder why I didn't run far away from this career after so many relapses. I suppose when you are in a situation, you often continue because you just can't see the way forward. A few months later, an agent secured a reference, which merely stated the dates I was employed with the firm. There was no information regarding how good a worker I was or any details about my character, even until the period of ill health, merely the dates of employment.

The travelling itself from the south-east of the city was demanding for me. I purchased a car, which still made the trip quite arduous, as I either had to take the M8 or the East End Route home and to the city. I had trouble sleeping, and I was worrying in the last few weeks about the completion of a job. One thing led to another, and I decided I would have to leave the job, as I was starting to feel stressed. Luckily enough, I was offered a position in Lanarkshire. This should have been straightforward, but by this time, I was becoming ill again. The symptoms were always the same: I stopped sleeping and started to worry about the work I was doing. Sometimes I was feeling good, and most people would be unaware that I was actually becoming ill.

The problem with this illness is that you are often unaware of the fact that your health has deteriorated. I had not been on medication for eleven months when this relapse took place. The same lack of awareness was present during the previous times that I had been ill, and sadly I lost all sense of reality. I distinctly remember thinking that night that somehow things would work out, and yet within a few hours, I was in another place altogether. I was in a state of confusion and unreality.

Sometimes I wish someone had intervened earlier, so that the stress and confusion would not have accumulated into the breakdowns that deprived me of the most important years of my life. But the onset of the illness itself is very difficult to detect, and in my case seemed to take place overnight.

There were days when reality shook the timbers of my fragile mind, and I wondered how on earth I could ever actually move forward in my life. Many dark days followed when I pondered the future, and daily activities seemed difficult to cope with at times. Initially, prior to the Scottish Nationalist Party being in power, each of the prescribed medications had to be paid for. The medications did stop the illness, but I relapsed three times when I was advised to stop them by the medical professionals. At one stage, the consultant considered starting me on lithium, and I was given a scan to see if my kidneys could tolerate this medication. For some reason, she decided against it, and I was given a reprieve.

The diagnosis of high blood pressure at the same time didn't surprise me, as I suppose I was a naturally type-A personality. However, over the last fifteen years, the high blood pressure has been dangerously high, and I did feel there was, at times, very little point to my life.

From my parents' perspective, it seemed difficult to understand that such events had taken place. My sister had not had such problems and I felt that there was an element of shame to it.

Some people never recover from the experience of being subjected to life on a psychiatric ward. You meet all kinds of people there from all walks of life. I have to say in all honesty that the people I met there, although broken, were some of the greatest people I had ever met in my life. It was, without a doubt, against all odds that I have managed to move forward at all. I started to see a pathway, albeit it was covered with weeds.

CHAPTER

Isolation and Unemployment

F or social psychology this year, I researched a project which
I chose myself on the propinquity effect with respect to the
maintenance of long-term friends after graduation and into the
middle years. The propinquity effect proposes that we tend to
form friendships with those closest in physical proximity to us.
Therefore, my friendship group was largely in agreement with the
propinquity effect, but if the friendship was particularly strong,
then individuals would maintain that friendship irrespective of
the distance involved. I had maintained friendships into the
middle years with most of my friends from university who had
distance from me later in life, either because of geography or
because they had married. In the case of the platonic friends,
it was no longer easy to meet alone.

After the first episode of illness fourteen years ago in 1999, I recovered quickly and returned to work, but it was during the relapse that life became very different for me and I was isolated from my world. I remember the occupational therapist coming to the house, asking me about my day, and devising plans about how I should spend it. Her idea was to watch the British soap opera *Eastenders* on television, in order to give me something to talk about and to learn about relationships. When I think of this now, it does make me feel quite amused about the patronising aspect of it and also the attempt at control. She assumed that this would give me a focus. I know that she had been trying to help, but that day I decided I would never allow anyone to dictate my thoughts again. In the early days, when I couldn't read, I just listened to music. I tried listening to the radio and then audio books, which helped immensely.

There had been an incident when I had been at a friend's house and I was telling another friend about the plot of *PS I Love You* (LaGravenese 2008). My friend had thought I was talking about people I knew. I suppose I realised then how much I was missing out on meeting people as I had very few friends at that point in my life. I think, looking back, that I was so full of guilt and fear that people would find out that in many ways, I was emotionally paralysed. These were the darkest days of my life. When I started going out again and returned to work in 2006, I found it difficult to relax in other people's company, in case they asked too many questions.

Looking back, I hadn't really thought about anything for many years other than finding work. Since 1994, I had been in various different firms and dealt with different characters. I was very quiet in those days and very much a people pleaser.

My life had continued throughout the years of illness with little social contact, especially with people my own age. Contract work was not good for me either at this stage, as there was a steep learning curve in familiarising myself with the work, the clients, and adjusting to different work practices. Life was tough in those days, and I found it difficult to move on from the past. I was still attached, in many ways, to my old firm, and I compared every place I went to it.

When I was released from contract in the summer of 2007, while working in a firm, I believe it was the beginning of the end for me. I remember being in Cala D'Or with my sister a few weeks later, and I think I was in a state of shock. My life was over; in many ways, I still believe this experience set the precedent for what was to happen in January 2008.

I was employed on another contract until January 2008, which was difficult because of the workload after a couple of months. In my working life, I can honestly say that I was not always treated with respect. If I could express the pain this has caused, it would be some form of release. Strangely enough, I had never cried during this period, because of the medication and also because these matters were not discussed at home.

A few weeks ago, I was listening to a sad song, and suddenly, for a few hours I released more tears than I had since 1999. The next day, I felt better than I had in many years. Bottling up is never a good idea.

It is difficult for people who have been ill in this way to integrate back into society because they are changed by the experiences they've had. Even travelling alone anywhere was challenging in the early days; I was afraid I may become ill in the street and be taken to a Glasgow hospital. Therefore, my life was always about being alone and not really feeling supported, other than by my family. Gradually, however, things improved, and with the help of a new friend, I grew in confidence and stayed out talking in cafes longer than I ever did previously in my working life. I started to discuss books and films, and I went to the cinema more often.

In Brandon Bays's *The Journey,* she asks you to speak to your younger self around an imaginary campfire (Bays 1999). I felt quite sad when I tried this process because my five-year-old and ten-year-old self were so full of hope and promise. I was a boisterous child who loved the outdoors, playing but also reading. I was a good all-rounder throughout my life. Perhaps I was a little too obedient to those in authority. I did develop an inferiority complex as a teenager, mainly because my hair was thinning from the age of fourteen. I remember looking at myself in mirror in the shadows, so I would not see the full extent of my hair loss. It has affected me throughout my life.

I worked very hard against all odds to become an accountant. I was the only one in my family to have attained this success. Sometimes I feel somewhat sad that my life and career were taken from me, even though I held on as long as I could. Regrets, yes I have many from those years. I could have relocated to England, but I suppose I didn't really want to leave at that time. Things changed so much that I had to rebuild my shattered personality and faith in humanity.

Perhaps one of the major factors in a person becoming ill from depression is unemployment. I suffered from depression throughout periods of unemployment. In the late nineteenth century, the term "depression" was used for the first time. There was a study carried out in a village in Austria, called Marienthal, where the majority of the community of working age were not able to work. This was because of the closure of a factory in the town. This study took place in 1931, prior to the Second World War.

Time is of the essence when we are at work, what with meeting deadlines and accounting for our time. Yet, when we are unemployed, the days seem endless. It is important to have structure to your day, as though you were still working. In this study, it was found that the unemployed people of Marienthal, when deprived of employment and severed from contact with people, lost the ability to structure their days. In fact, when asked about what they did on specific days in the previous weeks, they were unable to account for their time. If anything happened in the town, they did not hurry and merely continued their conversations. There was a gender difference, as the women of the town still had to prepare meals and generally look after the house (Jahoda, Lazarsfeld and Zeisel 2010).

The periods of solitude I experienced were also beneficial, as I was able to study and write about my experiences. I found solutions in books, in music, and in relationships. Some friends have become closer than relatives over the years; they have been there through good and bad times.

CHAPTER

Under Pressure

Different people have various methods of coping with pressure. There are many levels of threshold for stress, depending upon the activity required and the person involved. Uniqueness is an essential element of the individualistic experience. People of all classes and levels of income have reported the effects of stress, and yet it is difficult to pinpoint what it actually is and whether it really exists as an illness.

The term *stress* itself was used in the fourteenth century to relate to hardship or conflict. In the industrial age of the seventeenth century, the term referred to the pressure, for example, that a bridge could withstand. Later, in the 1920s, it was expanded to include the impact caused by negative life events. The term itself can mean different things to different people. It may be something in the individual's environment, like work stress, where they cannot cope with the demands required of them. Some other people consider stress is the effects of trying to cope, which may result in tiredness; thirdly, the transactional model of stress refers to an interaction between the two. People are said to make a cognitive appraisal on whether the event taking place will cause them stress.

The physiological experience which early man had when being charged by a predator resulted in the activation of the sympathetic branch of the autonomic nervous system. (ANS) The changes which take place are blood-pressure increases and changes in the blood-sugar level. There are also effects on the hormonal levels on the adrenal glands. The levels of cortisol are affected by the fight-or-flight response, which accelerates the ability to take action. Workplace stress is affected by office politics. Our cavemen ancestors would have taken flight if they were in danger, however, we have to remain, to maintain our jobs and therefore stress is induced, rather than being removed from the situation.

The problem with the terminology of stress is that it has now entered mainstream literature and the media. Therefore, a person under stress may consider that he or she is on the verge of a nervous breakdown. However, it is only when a person ceases to function on a daily basis that this situation applies; at that point, the person becomes the concern of medical professionals, who step in for crisis management. Once the medical intervention team are in place, the person is assumed to be on his or her way to recovery. Unfortunately, the wards in a general hospital are not entirely the place to recover from a nervous breakdown, as they can actually induce more stress, with overcrowding and the type of people around you.

Initially, I was in a single room and then with three other people. When visitors arrived, it was very stressful with so many people in the room. Sometimes at weekends, people would visit all day long, as the hours were relaxed, and there was a constant stream of people into the recovery rooms. Most patients were not there voluntarily or perhaps had started as voluntary patients and a section to detain them was placed in order afterwards, under the Mental Health Act. The patients were of all ages and evidently with very different character traits, a cross-section of the world. Sometimes it seemed like we would be there forever, living in this unreality.

I have to stress that the general hospital I stayed in was not like the priory. Being a patient there, it's as though your thoughts are no longer of any value, even to the staff, who may have little knowledge of your life. I often witnessed extreme lack of respect and refusal to call a medical doctor to examine a patient for a physical illness. This situation has actually been reported recently, in that many people who have suffered from physical problems in a ward for the treatment of mental health problems have actually been neglected and even died.

I remember having a chat with one of the nurses, in which he reviewed my mental state and general happiness. He asked me who my closest friends were, and I mentioned my Norwegian friend because I believed that to be the truth at the time, and I did see her more often in those days. He suggested that this was unusual and perhaps even delusional. This was evidently the perspective of someone with a very different life experience.

Three times in my life, I have had to be weaned off my medications, on the advice of the consultant. I can't express clearly enough how much fear that has induced in me at this time, because if the experiment didn't work, I could become ill again and lose years of my life. In 1999, the medication was stopped after six months, and within a year or so, I had become ill again. This happened on three different occasions over the fourteen-year period. It was probably written that it was my idea to try stopping the medications, but in those circumstances, the patient is like the human guinea pig, taking the advice of the doctors. Unfortunately, the concoction of drugs that another doctor prescribed made me feel worse than I ever had in my life.

For more than a year, I did not sleep, and I wanted my life to end. I lost all confidence, and my weight ballooned to sixteen stone. The second time, I was also encouraged to stop the medication, to see what happened; I had another relapse, and I lost five years of work and health as a result of it. I did survive almost a year without medication, but at the time, my life was out of balance because of my work life.

Today, I read an article in *The Metro* newspaper about the statistics of suicides of ex-military men and women. According to these statistics, twenty-two ex-soldiers take their own lives every day worldwide. For whatever reason, they find life outside of the army too difficult to cope with and feel bad enough about it to end their own lives. It is tragic that more is not done to help these soldiers adjust to their new environments, after they have been patriotic and fought for their countries. Evidently, what they had witnessed overseas had an impact.

I have felt tremendous despair over the years; however, I was lucky enough not to ever seriously think about taking my own life, even though at times it seemed impossible to go on. My life appeared to be over in January 2008, when I suffered the final breakdown. In fact, five years later, I still feel the same as regards my career in accountancy. I enjoyed my work in accountancy; however, it was very stressful at the end of my career. There was also a glass ceiling, and females found it harder to be promoted. Today I spoke to an agent who asked me the *why* question, as to the reason for my career break. I know that it is difficult for people to understand this absence, but what else can I say in response to this question? Honesty is the best policy. There were so many obstacles and brick walls that often there seemed no way to beat the system at all.

CHAPTER

12

Medication Side Effects and Insomnia

Since these periods of illness, it has been difficult for me to sleep. I am currently taking a small maintenance dose of medication. Different medications have caused more insomnia than others, but even now after five years, I still awaken through the night for at least an hour or so. Nowadays, it is no longer a curse, because I make good use of the time by working, and it probably isn't necessary for me to sleep through the night. With this comes acceptance that this is how my life is. In the last five years, I have tried various medications, which induced drowsiness throughout the day, sleeplessness at night, and promoted weight gain. There have also been other health problems, including high blood pressure, which may be directly related to the long-term medications I have taken over the last fourteen years.

Only fellow sufferers could understand how it feels to be awake while others sleep. Now I see it as an opportunity to work and find peace from the world. It is a time when there are no phone calls, and the silence is golden. In fact, sometimes I wish this feeling of peace would last throughout the day. Many people who are ill in this way are overmedicated, particularly in the early stages of crisis intervention, and then sometimes it is difficult to reduce the medications later, for fear of relapses. It is extremely sad to see people in the wards staring into space, unable to communicate with other people. There would be justification to use their medications, as they induce sleep, which is considered good for recovery. Each time I have become ill, my sleep was the first thing to be affected. The onset of the illness took place very quickly, sometimes overnight. However, looking back, it probably would have been brought about by extreme conditions, which I had worried about for months and sometimes years.

PART III

Solutions

In Venice.

My sister, Lena and me in Italy.

At Edinburgh Castle.

My sister,Lena in Sorrento,Italy.

My parents.

My friend, Elina Milano.

In the country.

Liver Building, Liverpool,England.

In Paris.

The castle in Malcesine, Italy.

CHAPTER

My Family and Recovery

My family have supported me through many difficult years, both financially and emotionally. This level of trust and confidence in them made me feel I could confide in them, although in general we did not talk much about the periods of ill health. My mother would come with me to the appointments with the consultant in the early years. This was a great help to me, particularly the first time I became ill. I admire her strength of character and belief in my recovery, even when it seemed quite a distance away. I have spent much more time with my parents and my sister than I would have expected because of the illness. It has been a great learning experience. It interests me to see how my parents keep themselves busy during the day. This, in turn, helped me form a structure to my days, even though I was not working for a lengthy period.

I was overcome by tiredness each time I tried to recover, which has been mainly because of the side effects of the medications. However, I have come to accept the limitations of my condition.

Without the support of my parents and my sister, it would have been impossible for me to recover as well as I did. They took the responsibility for the shopping and the housework, whilst my dad took care of the garden and general DIY projects. Most days I spent at home writing my reflections, which then became part of this book, and then latterly I was studying for my psychology degree with the Open University.

Although we have a large extended family, we dealt with our problems ourselves. There were many family occasions over the last fourteen years that I couldn't attend because of the illness. There were twelve deaths of family members during those years. It was very emotional to lose our relatives. Some younger cousins died too during this period, which was difficult to deal with.

I love my family. Although I do not see them as often as I would like, I learned a great deal from my aunts and uncles, and I have a deep bond of affection for my family.

There have been good times in between the periods of illness, and for the most part, I have managed well after each recovery.

When studying child development for my psychology degree, I became interested in attachment theory. It seemed probable that if you did not attach properly to your mother in infancy, you may face similar problems forming relationships later in your life. Yet this did not seem to correlate with my own life. I am very attached to my parents and my sister. I was a confident child who made friends easily. I believe that my mother was a great influence on me throughout my childhood. My parents brought me up with good family values and a great belief in Catholicism. My sister and I were told the importance of education at an early age. I had a close friendship with my older sister. In fact, she was in many ways the driving force in my life. If Lena achieved something, I wanted to follow in her footsteps. Evidently, with the age difference, there was a power relationship when we were younger. She took me everywhere on holiday when I was a student and could not afford to go abroad. After I became ill, she sacrificed many holidays abroad to support me.

Recovery after a breakdown is a slow process. It took a few experiences for me to realise the extent of the impact, both mentally and physically. I felt tired and lethargic. People would be having conversations around me that I couldn't follow. I would try to watch television programmes, and I found it difficult to follow the plots.

It is difficult to say when the point of recovery takes place. As someone who had dealt with facts and figures in my working life, I wanted to know how long the period of illness would last and when I could return to work. One doctor implied the recovery could be infinite, like the length of a piece of string, which really did not help, For me, though, the recovery initially was about adding structure to my day. There were always doctors and hospital appointments to attend to in the early days. Sometimes at these appointments, there was more reflection on the onset of the illness, rather than the recovery, which was a constant reminder of what had happened. I went to Mass most days at my local church, Holy Trinity and All Saints, and I started to feel better about going out and meeting people again.

I am a great believer in distraction techniques, whereby you take part in a different activity or talk about something other than what is troubling you. Some people believe in talking about their problems to solve them. However, I found distancing myself from them helped me better.

Each day that passed moved me towards better health.

I have changed dramatically over the past fourteen years. With each breakthrough, I have learned more about my ability to cope with any situation that arises. It has been frustrating at times, as I have wanted to work, but there have been many obstacles which have prevented me from achieving this goal. It is necessary to recover fully, prior to stepping back into the workforce, as it is necessary to be fit for work.

People can experience difficulty when trying to return to employment after a nervous breakdown, as it is difficult for the doctors to assess when you become well enough to work. It's not like a broken leg, which heals in a set period of six weeks; some people don't recover enough to return to the workforce. It is a Catch-22 situation because of the legal issues involved between the employer and the medical profession related to health and safety.

After a few experiences, now I feel secure knowing that I would be able to access the right help and also help myself. It is a point of acceptance, now that what has happened has been outwith my control. I wholeheartedly believe that you should take responsibility for your own health. However, because of the type of illness, you are often unaware of how ill you have become until there has been crisis-management intervention.

In many ways, it has been a solitary journey because although I've had my family around me during this lengthy period, I have had to experience the side effects myself and regain the confidence to master the basic things.

CHAPTER

Keep the Faith

I can honestly say that through the period of illness, despite everything that happened, I have managed to keep the faith. I believe that God chooses our path and that it is necessary to go with the flow and wait until we meet the right people to take us forward in our lives. Focusing on our own problems can prevent us from seeing the bigger picture and the impact it is having on other people's lives. We are all connected; it is necessary to reach out to those of us who are alone. Reflecting on this fourteen-year period of time, I now find it quite amazing that I have survived it. Yes, there were times when I wondered if I would ever find my way out of the darkness. I read Anne Rice's book, *Called Out of Darkness: A Spiritual Confession* about her religious beliefs and her loss of faith, followed by her return to the church (Rice 2009). Somehow, despite the tragedy of the last fourteen years, my devotion to the Blessed Virgin seemed to carry me through these difficult times. It has not been easy, and sometimes I questioned why this had happened to me.

The isolation was overwhelming at times. Because of the nature of my work and as a member of a large family, I always had people around me. Through this period, I had to adapt to being back home in my own town and being constantly asked about why I wasn't working. Although I enjoyed having time on my hands, I did not possess the money to enjoy the career break. Therefore, I had to amuse myself at home, watching films and devouring the books I never had the time to read when I was working. There was a time, just after the most recent period of illness, that I could not concentrate well enough to read for a lengthy period. As a result, I just listened to music instead. The lyrics of songs became very important to me, in particular the words of John Lennon and the Beatles. I have always identified with the song "Watching the Wheels", from the *Double Fantasy* album in which he spoke of his sabbatical period away from the music scene, when he became a house husband (Lennon, Double Fantasy 1980). I felt that I experienced similar feelings.

Depression is a strange kind of illness to have; unlike a physical illness, not many people have sympathy for you. Even those closest to you will tell you to "be a stronger person". I felt as though I had let everyone – including myself – down. In many ways, having a profession was a curse. Because of the complexity of the work, it was more difficult to return to work.

My religion is still very important to me. I am a practising Catholic, however, I believe that there are many spiritual ways of perceiving the truth. I have embraced other religions and philosophies whilst remaining true to my own faith. When I visited Lourdes in 2004, I believe that I experienced a miracle or at least a blessing at the Grotto of Massabielle. When I look at photos from that pilgrimage, I feel tremendous pain and suffering. In fact, until only recently, I found it difficult to view them. I was suffering... from the effects of the medication, from the weight gain, and from the slowness of my senses. In many respects, I was a person who had lost her spirit and was just going through the motions of everyday life.

I suppose that in my mind's eye, I still thought of myself as the accountant, but in reality, I felt like the spirit had almost left my body. From my knowledge of embodiment now, I know that coming to terms with my new appearance had a major impact on my self-esteem and my identity. Every day was a chore, but somehow, I could still smile for the cameras. There was sometimes a glimpse of my former self.

When I met the new consultant and she told me that she thought the illness was more of a depressive nature, I was overwhelmed. It was an awakening moment; the mutual respect carried me through the following years. However, I still felt that the obstacles to returning to work were insurmountable. After starting B12 injections for anaemia, I finally managed to secure some contract work. Outwith my family, my GP has been the greatest support to me throughout this difficult period. Without his care and attention, I am not sure that I would be in the same place emotionally.

Since I was a child, I have always prayed. The rosary was very important in our family. My mother still recounts the story of how her father knelt down to say the rosary every night. The mantra of the repetitions of the Hail Marys is very comforting, especially when a loved one is lost. The image of Mary has always given me some peace. Since I was a child, I visited the Shrine of Our Lady of Schoenstatt, which is now in the

Campsies in Scotland. It had previously been in the south side of Glasgow. The Schoenstatt convent movement was started by Father Josef Kentenich in Cologne, Germany, in 1914, just prior to the First World War. I have always prayed to Our Lady of Schoenstatt.

Last year in Munich, I attended Mass in the church of Frauenkirche. I had a vision of how it must have been for the German people standing in this church, praying that their country would not enter into a war. I also thought of those French and British people attending their churches at the same time and praying for peace. I remembered also a beautiful film called *Joyeux Noel* which came out a few years ago about the Christmas Truce, which told the story of the German and British troops who played football together on Christmas Day during World War One (Carrion 2006). On that day, in that sacred place, I had a sensation of being sprinkled with holy water from head to foot. Somehow, I believed then that my life would improve.

In my life, I consider myself blessed in comparison to other people. I have a great family, and throughout my time on this earth, I have made friends easily. Thanks to my parents, I had a fantastic education. Perhaps my greatest attribute is the gift which is innate in my family, the ability to speak to people of all creeds, races, and of different social groups as though we were brothers and sisters. This gift has made my life more vibrant and colourful, and I now know that there are many interesting things to be learned by opening the doors to people who are different to my own upbringing.

Once I could read again, I began to look into environmental causes for breakdown victims. I started my research by devouring books about the First World War. This was sparked by the film *Regeneration*, which affected me greatly when I first saw it in the cinema (Barker 2013). This was from a book by Pat Barker. Recently, I had researched the work of Hans Eysenck with respect to his studies on soldiers who were suffering from shell shock. As defined by the DSM-IV criteria, post-traumatic stress disorder is an extremely difficult diagnosis to receive because it can open the floodgates for compensation. The criteria for this diagnosis is that another person would have to have suffered in the same way in similar circumstances, but this does not take account of individual differences in temperament or the uniqueness of human experience.

In the First World War, experimentation was done on soldiers suffering from shell shock. Trench warfare was an experience many people could not adapt to, especially if they witnessed the death of their fellow soldiers. Amongst other places, soldiers in World War One convalesced at Craiglockhart in Edinburgh; some of these men were later featured in the film *Regeneration* (Mackinnon 1997). Amongst the soldiers at Craiglockhart were the famous war poets Wilfrid Owen and Siegfried Sassoon, the latter of whom became a conscientious objector and a peace campaigner.

The First World War, being a land and sea battle fought mainly in the fields of France or off the coast of Great Britain affected everyone's lives. Even though some returned from the Second World War to live full lives, settling down to have their families, they never forgot what they had witnessed. Others, scarred forever never recovered from the experience. Still others were shot at dawn for desertion; now, we would know that they were actually suffering the effects of shell shock. Even a century later, many of these soldiers have not been pardoned. Today's wounded Gulf War veterans can count on assistance from charitable organizations that provide (or facilitate access to) needed services not provided by the state, such as Help for Heroes (*www.helpforheroes.org.uk*).

CHAPTER

The Mystery of the
Light Concept

When my former teacher, Benny Timpson, reviewed my story for the first time, he pointed out that I had mentioned the lightness and the darkness often in the songs that I had referenced and in the narrative. I was struck with the duality of polarities. I had been attracted to songs that referenced light. In the Bible, Jesus is referred to as the "light of the world". Jesus mentions that he is "the Way, the Truth and the Light" and that no-one can reach the Father without him. In the fourth Mysteries of the Rosary, which were incorporated by Pope John Paul II, the Mysteries of Light again enforces this power of God.

As the band Simple Minds says in their song "See the Lights", you can "see the light shining in front of you" (Kerr and Burchill 1991). At the end of the day, when natural light fades, we must rely on the less-beneficial artificial light to see our way.

Because the light generated by gas lamps is far more subdued than modern artificial light, people in ages past were unable to work into the late hours as we do now. Just as physical light adds to the quality of an environment, emotional lightness also enhances the quality of our relationships. This "lightness" in demeanour and attitude can also create the sensation of feeling "lighter" in certain company. By contrast, when someone talks about their problems all the time, this introduces an emotional heaviness to a relationship.

In social psychoanalytical psychology, splitting techniques emphasise how we see aspects of our lives in good and bad or lightness and darkness, therefore the concept of dual polarity.

We see better in the light, and we have a different field of vision and perspective. We are liberated by knowledge, even when we recognise that we are only hearing half-truths. Some people go through their lives without worrying too much about the future, whereas others spend a great deal of time wondering how they will make it through the next week.

There is nothing more inspiring than to see a person whose light shines radiantly from his or her face. These are the people who have faith in God or the universe, and their smile reaches their eyes instantly.

CHAPTER

Music, Literature, and the Movies

P rior to the time when children learn the spoken language of their own culture, they communicate with their parents through a pseudo-language, smilling and crying. Music is very important to them at this time too.

When people become ill through despair, they become more involved with their own recurring thoughts and problems. In many ways, they tend to withdraw from those around them. This withdrawal also has a rebound level on the amount of activity they are taking part in. As a result their problems become their life. In extreme cases, the individual may start to experience disturbed thoughts or hallucinations; whether this is because of the influx of chemicals in the body or because of the stress (or vice versa), no one actually knows for certain. The dopamine and serotonin levels are affected by the release of adrenaline and noradrenalin into the bloodstream from the constant "flight-or-fight" response. Serotonin levels are low in a person with depression; they may require antidepressants to improve their mood. Conversely, in psychosis, high dopamine levels require medication to reduce the level back to normal.

Music has been used to heal people for centuries. Nowadays, music therapy can help people with a wide range of illnesses. From a social constructive perspective, lyrics have the ability to change a person's ideas about special concepts. Some music has been political and has a definitive message for change, while other music is soothing. The music therapist uses emotional, social, and spiritual methods to help the patients improve their health.

Music had always been a major influence in my life, but in 1999, it became all-important. There were days I could do little else but listen to music. From 2000 until 2004, my longest period of isolation ,I revisited the old songs of my youth. But it wasn't until 2008 that I realised the significance of the way in which music could promote good vibrations. Music can actually help people control their thoughts. Neurolinguistic programming (NLP) also employs music as a therapeutic tool. By learning to associate a traumatic memory with a favourite song, for example, NLP patients can thereby reshape that association from negative to positive. The radio is also an excellent distraction for people who have been ill, as it helps them hear the daily news and maintain a sense of reality.

According to the Law of Attraction, the state of love is considered to have the highest vibrational energy. Being "in the highest vibrational state" means that you will attract more abundance into your life. For this and many other reasons, it is from a place of love that I live most of the time. So, in order to stay in a good state of mind, I tend to be particular about the music I listen to.

I believe the music an individual listens to does influence him or her, particularly the meaning of the lyrics. The Internet, via sites such as YouTube, has changed the way we experience music. Now we have access to music and videos from all over the world.

Since the last breakdown, I read many books by Jack Canfield. His *Success Principles* book is always close at hand, in order to revisit certain passages (Canfield 2005). The greatest thing about this book is that it is said to include all the information he had learned over thirty years in seminars and from books. Therefore, it is only necessary for the individual to buy one book. I first encountered him in the film, *The Secret*. I was impressed by his quiet demeanour which in comparison with the more aggressive types of coaches, was refreshing. In early 2008, one of Jack's American consultants gave me a complimentary call. She was very helpful and was able to help me resolve various issues about my career. She suggested that I make a complete change to a more caring profession. I was still attached to the fact that I was a chartered accountant, with hopes that I would return to my high-flying career. However, speaking to her led me to various life-coaching articles and finally to study for a degree in psychology with the Open University. I chose this course of study in the hopes that it would help me gain greater awareness about the possible roots of my illness. This was the greatest experience of my life.

But it was also a very lonely experience. Studying with the Open University was a very solitary time. No one in the family really appreciated the amount of work that was required. For someone like me, who couldn't read for almost a year after each breakdown, studying this subject at this level was a remarkable achievement. Initially, I thought I would only study one module at a time, but now three years later, I only have one course to complete. There were four modules, including social psychology, cognitive psychology, child development, and exploring psychology. The degree helped me to find solutions and to pinpoint various areas in which my life had become unbalanced, a goal I had set when I made the decision to study for this degree.

Another influence was the writings of Paulo Coelho. I have read most of his books over the last decade, and I was fortunate enough to meet him a few years ago at the Scottish Exhibition Centre in Glasgow, when he had released *The Witch of Portobello*. I thanked him for writing *The Zahir: A Novel of Obsession.* My favourite book of his is *By the River Piedra, I Sat Down and Wept,* set in the town of Lourdes in the Pyrenees. Another of his books, *The Pilgrimage: A Contemporary Quest for Ancient Wisdom,* about Santiago de Compostela and the Camino, led me to meeting my good friend, Elina from Florida. She has been supportive over the last decade and visited me here in Scotland almost a year ago.

I am not sure why I have spent most of my life in the search for meaning and purpose. In the early days of being a chartered accountant, I thought I had found the career that would give me a good lifestyle. However, this did not really enhance my life. As with anything else, I enjoyed some aspects of the job, but it wasn't exactly what I felt I was born to do. Around this time, after reading *The Passion Test: The Effortless Path to Discovering your Destiny* (Attwood 2008), I realised that my true passion was for writing, music, and film media. The lyrics of Beatles songs had been meaningful to me since I was a child, as was the music of Elvis Presley. I suppose that we all identify with music and lyrics for one reason or another. When listening to Presley's "In the Ghetto" recently, I realised the impact this song had on me as a child. Perhaps, in his lyrics, my social conscience was born.

In the movie *Music and Lyrics,* the protagonist Alex Fletcher (Hugh Grant) states that music is more important than the lyrics. Sophie Fisher (Drew Barrymore) challenges him by explaining that if music is the visual representation of the person, the lyrics allow you to see their soul. She then goes on to say that in order to see the complete character of a person, both the music and lyrics are essential.

Culturally and traditionally, music has been important throughout history. For me, it is the combination of the lyrics and the singer/songwriter's performance that makes the most impact. For example, knowing that when Elvis Presley was going through a divorce when he recorded his *Aloha from Hawaii* television special in 1973, one can imagine how his painful, personal challenges influenced his choice of songs at the time. Therefore, because it reflects our feelings and emotions, certain music is important at different times in our lives.

Ever since I was a child, I have loved the movies. My mother could name many Hollywood stars, even the more obscure ones. This always impressed me as a child, and I'm pleased that this has been a gift she passed on to me. In comparison to times past, movies released today, in my opinion, focus too much on the less-important aspects of life and sensationalise violence in order to achieve box-office success. Despite these disturbing trends, one can usually find a good message in most movies and perhaps a worthwhile scene or two, which makes the two hours spent seem worthwhile.

Musicals have always interested me. Recently, I watched the beautiful film *August Rush,* starring Jonathan Rhys Meyers, one of the finest films I have ever seen. It is a story of fate and destiny, and the concept of passing your talents on to the next generation. The music is very important to the characters in the film. The title character, August Rush, is a child who was called Heaven by his mother. His parents are musicians: the father in a rock band and the mother a classical cellist. They meet one night in New York and then separate, and August ends up in an orphanage. He never gives up hope that he will meet his parents and that somehow the music will reunite them.

CHAPTER

John Lennon and "Imagine"

I have loved the Beatles since I was a child. My parents were not fans; I don't remember them playing their music in the house. Perhaps I learned of their music on my sister's radio. By 1966, when I was born, they were almost moving on to their final years in the band and to their respective solo careers. Even now, I remember all the words of their songs, even if I don't play some of them for a while. I believe that I experienced a transformational change in my health through listening to the Beatles's lyrics and John Lennon's solo work.

I was in my third-year biology class at St Patrick's High School when the teacher announced that John Lennon had died.

I had been listening to his new album, *Double Fantasy,* for several weeks and had followed (Lennon and Ono 1980) *The John Peel Sessions* with John and Yoko prior to this tragic event. I'll never forget this defining moment in my life and how much of an impact it made on me at a young age.

This album meant even more to me as the years passed by. Little did I know that by 1999, I would also be "watching the wheels" later in my life, just like one of John's songs on the album (Lennon, Double Fantasy 1980). I lost count of the times friends and family asked me how I could stay at home all day. The perception was that I spent the day simply "staring at four walls". Granted, while accurate some days, this description struck me as cruel as well. In those days, it wasn't easy for me to participate. The void seemed endless and impossible to fill. So, at that time, this song reflected my life, as it does today. Even though I managed to make it back onto the merry-go-round, somehow it was not the same experience, because I had transformed and I no longer belonged there.

As I write this, it's been thirty-three years since John passed. Through the lyrics of his songs, he remains as a constant in my life, a trusted spiritual companion and advisor. In many ways, he is a guiding spirit who inspires me to see sense in a world which is often difficult to comprehend. There is so much to admire in his integrity and sense of justice.

After visiting Mendips, his childhood home in Liverpool, I felt a stronger connection with him. Perhaps I was attracted to his incredible intelligence, sense of humour, creativity, or intensity. Maybe it was his Celtic roots, as his ancestors were from Ireland. Mendips was a house much like my own home. The kitchen had an extension where visitors other than the vicar and the doctor would enter the house. When I looked out of his bedroom window, I tried to imagine what he saw in that view that inspired his ascent to international success.

What do I love about him so much after all these years? I believe my appreciation began in his early days. I admired his quirky sense of humour, his wonderful accent, his ability to always laugh at himself or the world. Mainly, it was the John who wanted to change the world with his peaceful revolution that I loved. I was also intrigued by the more serious side of his character he expressed on his solo career. In those years, when I found it difficult to socialise often, his music guided me and made me experience the presence of God. With his example and inspiration, my healing began.

The song "Borrowed Time" (from the posthumous album *Milk and Honey)* made me realise that I would have to change my life. I was growing older; life was passing me by. There was a sense of urgency to start over again and actively participate in life. I was conscious of the fact that there had been periods when I had lost contact with people. Although I missed various opportunities through not working, the song made me realise that I had evolved in a different way. In certain respects, it was good to grow older. As much as I would have preferred to have not been ill, I had learned so much from the experience.

Many people thought that John had lost belief in God, but I believe (particularly in the latter years of his life), he was very close to the Higher Power.

So many songs like "Mind Games" and "Love" helped me understand that there were answers to my own life and another way of looking at the problem (Lennon, Mind Games 1973; (Lennon, Love 1970). *Double Fantasy* was an album of beautiful love songs between John and Yoko, which sadly will always be associated with the tragedy to follow (Lennon and Ono 1980).

"In My Life" will always be very close to my heart. In many ways, he expressed so eloquently the same thoughts I could not express myself as I had once found a new love which surpassed all those people that I had loved before.

My favourite photo of John and Yoko is the one in which he is handing her some flowers – a simple expression of love that, for me, still speaks volumes.

I have had many influences in my life, and I enjoy most types of music. Every time I visit church for Mass, I light a candle for John Lennon, to thank him for being my mentor throughout the lonely years when many friends disappeared – and for changing my perspective so that those absent friends never interested me again.

Throughout the periods when I was taken off medicine, his song "Cold Turkey" meant a lot to me. The pain he expressed in the lyrics mirrored my experiences at the time (Lennon, Cold Turkey 1975). No one else could understand the loss of the safety net or the fear that if you became ill again, it would be a long way back.

I could write many chapters about his songs, but it is John Lennon's strength, good humour, and keen intelligence that keep him in my heart and my soul to this day.

In my opinion, "Imagine" by John Lennon is perhaps the most important theme of the twenty-first century (Lennon, Imagine 1971). Written in 1971, it has travelled through time to give meaning to our lives. It is a song of peace and of love. Decades after it was written, the banking crisis, the credit crunch, and the recession in Britain brought about changes some people did not want in their lives. Throughout the world, countries were in crisis. People were losing their homes and their ways of life. Previously in Britain, since Mrs Thatcher, the then-prime minister encouraged working and middle-class families to buy their own homes; property has grown in importance to people. With the shortage of council homes then, everyone tended to buy a house with the finance raised from mortgages. In order to compete with their neighbours, they had to buy a new car, travel abroad to some exotic holiday destination, and buy every new gadget on the market. There are many people who are still obsessed with materialism and who remained in employment throughout the recession.

However, a majority of people are now becoming aware that they bought into a system whereby they were on the treadmill, working harder and longer hours to pay for the luxurious lifestyle. They worked extremely long hours, spent less time with their families, and put the children in nurseries. Sometimes, marriages broke up and the children had emotional problems. We live as products of a time when it was popular to stay at home at the weekends to watch movies; everyone has clutter from collecting videos and DVDs. Nowadays, we realise the importance of mixing with other people and taking regular exercise, rather than sitting around watching TV on the sofa all evening. As a result of this new practice, the charity shops are booming.

When I was at school in the 1980s, the video recorder came into existence. Looking back, it is hard to imagine how we all became embroiled in this practice of staying home to watch videos. Since Eckhart Tolle wrote *The Power of Now,* many books have adhered to these principles, whereby people are advised to live in the now. For a while, I took comfort living for the present moment, but there was much to resolve from the past, and planning for the future became more important. It is necessary to focus on the future and reflect on our past without dwelling there. There are benefits of living in the now. However, I see it rather as a place of no return, where we detach ourselves from the warmth of human experience, whereas the message of Utopia, as presented in Lennon's "Imagine" does not ask us to forget the past. Instead, it asks us to have "faith in the future" as in the song "Mind Games" (Lennon, Mind Games 1973).

I still love John Lennon after all these years. Whenever I have felt alone in this world, his music made me realise that he thought in the same way I did. He had a great awareness and empathy for the world's problems. He will always be a source of information and inspiration for me, and I believe that he has shown us the way to peace and salvation.

Through my own periods of darkness, I started to imagine how I could manage to remove the obstacles and push back the barriers to allow me enough freedom to experience a normal life. Over the years, I have felt imprisoned by the castle walls. At times, the future has seemed bleak. I have not had great success with meditation. Because I tend to view the world through words, not images, visualisation was difficult for me initially. Several years ago, I started to keep vision books (what we would have called "scrapbooks" when I was a child). I would cut and paste beautiful images of places I wanted to visit or experiences I wanted to have. There were recurring themes throughout this period which were represented in these books. In the early days, I was just looking for someone to share my life and some suitable employment.

But latterly, I have started to dream again. I imagine travelling to New York and Mexico, and to Rio de Janeiro to see the Christ the Redeemer statue. I first heard about these vision books from John Assaraf in the film *The Secret*. In the film, John found that he was living in the same house as he had cut out of a magazine and pasted onto the vision board (R. Byrne 2006). It was like this happened by magic!

Several themes have arisen from the maintenance of the vision books in my life. Strangely enough, about three years ago, I started to include pictures of Liverpool in the vision books. Since then, I have visited the city nine times in two years.

Development of the right side of the brain and the creative side of a person's life is essential to dealing with living in society today. Every day, we are bombarded with sad news on the TV and the radio. For this reason, I rarely watch TV now and avoid reading the newspapers. When I do read this information, I try to remain detached and impartial to it. Visualization techniques are essential when we have to imagine the life that we want in the now and in the future.

There are many visualization techniques in order to imagine what you would like to materialise in your life. Some people do not know what they would actually want in their lives. In the initial stages, it takes someone to point them in the right direction. As human beings, personal space is very important. Sometimes, interference from other people prevents you from living your own reality. Friends and family can place restrictions on your life because they did not have the confidence or courage to walk the road you wish to embark on. In times of trouble, it may become necessary to shift the goalposts and look for alternative routes.

Anyone can recreate his or her own life and choose the pathway which brings the greatest joy. The creation of our lives starts with three steps: ask God for whatever it is we desire, believe we will receive it, and accept that it will take place. There is, of course, a time delay in receiving what we ask for. Throughout the fourteen years when I was ill and unable to work, I had to listen to health professionals, family members, job-centre advisors, employers, and many others who would tell me I needed to take a lesser job and that my best years were behind me. These people had little knowledge about the power of the mind and the subconscious to repair and heal itself. Self-healing comes from within and with the help of prayer. For me, the simple act of listening to uplifting music feeds my soul. It can make the difference between having a good or a bad day. Certain tools like the Sedona Method are useful to release emotions and to allow people to stay in a place of peace. It is from this mind-set that wonderful experiences and people are attracted into your life.

The state of love is easy to attain. It can involve being in love, receiving love, or giving love. Focusing on the people and places we love sets a vibration of peace and gratitude, and this actually changes how we see the world. Evidently, change is necessary from within before we can try to change the world.

CHAPTER

Liverpool

On 9 October 2010, in honour of what would have been John Lennon's seventieth birthday, I travelled to Liverpool with my sister for the first time to see the unveiling ceremony of the European Peace Monument erected in his honour. It seemed strange to realise that he was only two years younger than my father. Of course, John would always remain young in my eyes. When he died, he was only six years younger than I am as I write this. His son, Julian Lennon, and his ex-wife, Cynthia Lennon, were at the ceremony that day. We took the Magical Mystery Tour bus, which was a special tour for John's birthday. We visited places that were important to him, including Strawberry Fields, Mendips, and Penny Lane. I fell in love with Liverpool that day. I knew that I would always return to this beautiful city. For some reason, over the next two years, several opportunities to visit Liverpool became available to me.

I found some vitality and a sense of purpose by visiting this exciting city. I love that the bus drivers can all sing "Penny

Lane" amongst other Beatles songs (Lennon and Mc Cartney 1967). I love that the people there call you "love". In the city of Liverpool, I found many genuine people who would go to any lengths to help you if they could.

Through my love of the Beatles and John Lennon, I have met many interesting people, and my life has been enriched as a result of it.

For me, John Lennon's music was essential to help me through the last fourteen years. In times of despair, his words and music made me feel less alone. I took comfort from knowing that he understood pain and loss, even although he had achieved great fame. It made me feel that perhaps one day, I too would move forward, find peace and hopefully even love.

After all this time, I still love John Lennon because he was able to stand up for what he believed in. He loved life and dedicated the latter part of his life to social change and the civil rights movement. It is remarkable now to reflect and realise what he achieved in a short timeframe. He was a bright star, too bright to stay too long.

Once you visit, there is something about Liverpool that just has the power to change your life forever. As a Beatles fan, it was always on my list of things to do before I died. But even I could never have predicted the contentment I would receive from visiting the city. One of the things that I loved about the Beatles was their ability to always make me laugh. In my mind, they will always be four evangelists dedicated to spreading the word of Jesus: "All you need is love", a simple and powerful message. Perhaps nowadays we need the Beatles and their message of love more than ever before. This is a world of austerity and draconian measures. It is a place of materialism, where people do not look for the spirit in their lives. We need to learn to laugh at ourselves like they did then, and to enjoy life again.

The second you walk in the Albert Dock in Liverpool, you feel an energy force. Perhaps this is because of the importance of the city in Imperial Britain. With its diverse cultural roots and its ability to laugh at itself, Liverpool stands as a beacon of light to me that is always calling me home.

For me, the most amazing realisation from my 9 October 2010 visit for the dedication of the monument is that people came to Liverpool from all over the world to celebrate his life. I started 2012 in Liverpool with Elina, my friend from Florida. Liverpool was instrumental in affecting change in my life. I had previously felt quite old and that the die had been cast for the future because of my illness. I wont there and realised that the Beatles fans were still going to watch live music in the Cavern Club. On 8 December 2012, I returned to stand at the Peace Monument at 8.00 p.m. to reflect on the life of a great man. It was a very moving night. I was very happy to take part in this event, one of the absolute highlights of my year.

CHAPTER

The New Thought Movement

In 2006, *The Secret* was released as an unadvertised book and a DVD (R. Byrne 2006). However, in a Borders bookstore in Buchanan Street, I came across the book, and it has changed my life. Some critics of the series later complained that people were required to take action in order for certain wishes to materialise in their life. I returned to *The Science of Getting Rich,* by Wallace D. Wattles, a one-hundred-year-old instruction manual for obtaining abundance in one's life. He defines a rich life as one that is filled with abundance or great joy (Wattles 2007). Many of the books in this genre – including *The Key* by Joe Vitale, *The Secret Things of God* by Dr Henry Cloud, which relates *The Secret* (R. Byrne 2006) book to the Bible (Vitale 2009; Cloud 2009) – are important to me.

The New Thought Movement was started by the Christian Scientists at the turn of the twentieth century. Horatio W Dressers's *A History of the New Thought Movement* explained how it was the generation after the Great War that gave birth to the new enlightenment of the New Thought Movement (Dresser 2008). Initially, it was a method by which one could explain the reasons the war happened but also to ensure that people could move forward from it. As the nineteenth century enjoyed a scientific revolution in which many new inventions were incorporated into everyday society, the world seemed to distance itself from the divine and became more materialistic. Evidently, the evolutionary perspective did move people away from the spirituality and closer to materialism and living in the now, without the concept of heaven and hell. Although evolution was a breakthrough at the time, in many ways, life became less magical and more explainable by the wonders of science.

From Germany, the idealistic thought movements spread throughout Europe and eventually to the United States. This movement explained that through our own thoughts, we could transcend our life experience by creation. Therefore, the inner world was more important; If certain aspects of our life were focused upon, we could actually recreate the external world through visions of what we wished for. Mental healing was considered to be brought about by employing the methods of thought control. The masters of the movement returned to look at the Bible to review the methods by which Jesus healed people. Because of the Reformation, some people no longer required priests to make sense of the teachings of Christ. Psychical research became more important too at this time. Spiritualism was thought to be a defence against materialism in the nineteenth century. In today's society, many are returning to embrace the principles and teachings of the New Thought Movement. One of the concepts of this movement is that the right teacher will appear when required.

The methods used are those of intuition and the concentration on the inner light as guidance of the soul. Originally, this movement was called the Mental Healing Movement. The old thoughts, those focused on the atonement of sins, misery, and the darkness, were considered pessimistic. In contrast, the New Thought Movement focused on the positive aspects of life and the fulfillment of future promise. They emphasised that man had free will and that the previous focus on hereditary had been unhealthy. The Law of Attraction then became important and clarified that it was the inner state which could draw people and things to it. As one of the laws of the universe, it has existed from the beginning of time. Therefore, once the inner state was altered, a person could effectively change his or her own life. At the turn of the twentieth century, psychology, inspired by these original philosophical teachings, was emerging and claiming its own place.

As a practical tool, the principles of the New Thought Movement can alleviate the symptoms of the people who are suffering from depression and other mental disorders. It is a method of thought control by which the individual is encouraged to focus on good thoughts to transcend bad times. In the early days, when I learned this through the many books I had read, it seemed quite difficult to change my train of thought. However, with practise, I learned a simple method: by channelling through my moods, I could then select a better one on a permanent basis. It is possible to do this by focusing on good thoughts or music. I should note that this approach does take practise and does not happen overnight, and the changes in the moods are gradual.

Nowadays, because I know how to maintain this level of optimism, I no longer succumb to sadness, even when a particularly unhappy event has taken place. The radio has an important role to play with the choice of channels. The use of changing channels on the radio to listen to uplifting music or perhaps a documentary may alter someone's mood.

Love exists at a higher frequency of energy state. This can be the feeling of being in love with another person or the unconditional love felt for a child or a parent. At this point, it is necessary to understand that love comes from within; love is a state of energy that can be attained without the presence of another human being. From this powerful state, individuals will start to attract whatever they desire into their lives. I have not attracted great monetary wealth, but when measured in terms of an abundance of good health and a happy family life, I am truly wealthy.

I listen to Smooth Radio here in the UK, a station that plays '70s hits and easy-listening music too. It is impossible to remain in a low mood when listening to these songs. However, there is a place for sad songs too; these often help people to release emotions that may be causing problems. Music is an excellent, affordable way to manipulate one's mood, so it's a good option for people on a low income. If you are looking to enhance your feelings of love, then a feel-good movie could magnify these feelings for two hours, if watched with purpose.

As demonstrated in *The Celestine Prophecy* when a person gives love to another person (even with a smile or shared laughter), the energy of both individuals involved increases. In the film, this was demonstrated when people focused on each other, sending love or good vibrations. In this way, the energy was passed from one to another. As the intensity of this love grows, they are able to reach a higher level of consciousness. Once reached, this place of peace is priceless; I am reminded of this sensation whenever I listen to Belinda Carlisle's "Heaven on Earth" song (Noweles and Shipley 1987). People who have practiced this technique, myself included, know that it is a waste of time to talk about what might have been; we know that we can reconstruct the circumstances we have enjoyed in the past. Some people may need to explore changes in their medications, as these can interfere with attaining this level of consciousness.

Many have experienced positive results through the use of mesmerism. Some were cured and able to achieve this state of love and serenity by holding their hands. In that both feature eye contact and a transference or energy and warmth, mesmerism is similar to hypnotism, but there are differences. When one is mesmerised, there is no loss of control, whereas when one is hypnotised, the individual will be in a trance state. Action still needs to be taken, but a person's life can change quite dramatically through these procedures.

CHAPTER

Gratitude

The concept of gratitude has been instilled in me all of my life by my parents, grandparents, teachers, and the clergy. This was reinforced some five years ago, when I read *The Secret.* It is of the greatest importance to give thanks for what you have already received and for what you will receive in the future.

There are many things for which I am grateful in my life. (Some are too personal to mention here.) However, in conversation with my friend the other day, I realised how grateful I was for the divine power in my life. For some reason, I needed to suffer this period of illness and be isolated from the world before I could transform into a new person altogether.

So the gratitude that I feel is, firstly, for the sacrifices my parents made in order to bring me into the world and look after me in good and bad times. I have great gratitude to my father for working hard and my mother for providing a nice home and sound morals. I thank them for allowing me the greatest gifts of my life: my faith and my education. If it is true that we choose the family we want to be born into prior to birth, then I made the right choice. Secondly, I thank my sister, Lena, who has offered the greatest support of my life. Even with our great struggles, she has stood by me all these years. I apologise to her; her sense of duty meant that she sacrificed her own happiness to support me through the last fourteen years. I cannot begin to tell you how much pain this still causes me.

For myself now, I ask nothing but good health and a way to support myself. Sometimes, I believe that I must have committed terrible crimes in a past life for which I must now atone. I suffered as I watched my friends find husbands and have children. I watched as the years passed me by. As my own career stagnated, I watched colleagues being promoted above me. Nevertheless, I have been blessed in many ways with a great family and many wonderful friends who came into my life.

CHAPTER

The Importance of Change

S ocial constructionism suggests that we must be critical about our perspective on the world and other people's viewpoints. Therefore, it opposes the scientific, empirical methods. Our viewpoint in the world is mainly dictated by the historical time in which we live and the culture to which we belong. This theory proposes that meaning is constructed between two people or that a person watching a film or reading a book can experience this interaction.

The culture in which we are born already has conditions and rules for learning the language and culture of your place of birth. It is considered that language is a precondition for thought because we develop it prior to our concepts and ideologies being formed. Traditionally, psychology had considered language to be passive.

From its origins in the works of North American, British, and European writers, social constructionism came into being some thirty years ago, exploring concepts which initially emerged from philosophical teachings. In medieval times, all decisions on thoughts, truth, and morality were made by the church. Later, during the Age of Enlightenment, the search for truth and the nature of reality became of ultimate importance.

The theories and perspectives embraced by people are fluid phenomena at best. There is rarely a true status quo. In discursive psychology, the method by which people use everyday language is studied. People use interpretative repertoires to tell their story. They also develop subject positions as to their own beliefs and attitudes towards a subject. The application of the social constructionist approach is that effectively, we can change our opinions in the interactive process with another person. Perhaps we may read a book or watch a film about a topic that we know little about, and it changes the way we think. Evidently, our opinions and attitudes have evolved from different sources, including our families, peers and close friends.

We can change the way we think as individuals, thereby changing society as a whole. Active change can be brought about by manipulation of the belief systems which may have been held for most of a person's lifespan. Society itself can change by critical incidents; sometimes the slight event alters perception, causing a seismic shift. In Lewis Grassic Gibbons's *Sunset Song*, (Grassic Gibbon 2006), he explains how the First World War changed Scotland when many of the songs and traditions were lost forever. By the end of the book, the blues have replaced traditional Celtic music as the preferred form of music. The old world, in this way, was lost forever. From a social constructionist perspective, the lyrics of songs are very powerful. Some songs are played repetitively on the radio or by individuals who like the words; this alone can bring about change in individuals and society.

When TV came to the UK in 1950s, the great aspects of the United States, especially the movies and musicals from Hollywood, filtered through. However, along with the musicals, it also brought about a period of change, as British society was influenced by American- style gangster movies. With the many television and Internet channels today, life has become very complex. Now, thanks to the never-ending variety and availability, one could watch violent cop movies all day long if he preferred. It does not take an expert to extrapolate how the effects of this behaviour might alter the consciousness of an obsessive individual. Likewise, romantic films also alter one's perceptions of the world by projecting unrealistic expectations onto people, rendering their own relationships very dull in comparison. But on the other hand, the positive impact of these romantic films is immeasurable; for two hours, we feel love vicariously through these films and hope that someone could come along for us. Ultimately, one does not need the Hollywood version of love and romance to be happy; life can still be exceptional with the right attitude.

As a result of the influence of movies and television, the world has become ever more homogenous by the day, no matter what country you live in. There are McDonald's and Burger King restaurants in thousands of cities all over the world. In my opinion, it is uniqueness we should be encouraging in individuals, not conformity. This should be embraced in every city of every country in the world.

Uniqueness of the individual is what promotes creativity. It separates the leaders from the pack. It is time we valued these skills in people, rather than some mass-produced regurgitation of facts and trends. They should move forward in true adventurer style, like Columbus and the conquistadors, who perhaps initially were inspired by the chance of recreating a new world and saving the souls of others by the message of Christianity. That said, the concept of conversion was noble but utterly misguided; every race has a different way of expressing *their* love for God.

Destiny

I n 1916, my grandfather was an able seaman on the *King George V* ship in the Battle of Jutland during World War I. Surprisingly, he survived this experience. He returned home, then several years later, he married my grandmother, and they raised a family of seven. His father had twice tried to settle in Scotland from Northern Ireland, in order to improve conditions for his family. My maternal grandmother was born in Scotland to Northern Irish parents, and she met and married my grandfather, who had also relocated from Northern Ireland. Had any of these events not taken place, my parents, my sister, and I would not be here today.

Is this a matter of chance or destiny? Over the years, I have pondered this question, and I believe we each have our own purpose for being here for a certain period in the specific time we live on this earth. Destiny is a concept which states that the events in our lives unfold because of predetermination, not free will. Some spiritualists suggest that before we are born, we exist in heaven, and we decide which families we will join in order to facilitate the work we are required to do here on earth. To most people, this would seem unrealistic, as many children unfortunately do not make it into the world and others are mistreated. It is obvious, though, that we are all connected as a species, and this has actually intensified, even more so now, thanks to the Internet.

Recently, many people from my past have resurfaced without much effort on my part to find them. Some of them had disappeared from my life long before I was ill, and yet now, it seems like they have never been away. Some were friends for only a short period of time, and yet they made more of an impact than those who were in for the long haul. It is almost as if they appeared by magic, ready to take me to the next phase of my life. In the years following 2004, when I left my office, I still wanted back to the life I once enjoyed. How many times did I walk through Glasgow, wishing to see an old friend but to no avail? The time was not right. As always with the universe, it is necessary to accept the ebb and tide. Sometimes, the answers we seek lie in unexpected places – the right person, the right book, or the right song. Sometimes there is more help available in these sources than in speaking with a therapist, who may or may not have any direct experience with your situation.

23

Social Media and Connectedness

The Internet has changed our lives forever. It became important to me some ten years ago when I started using the Easy Internet Cafes, prior to accessing it at home. I had many friends whom I had met when I lived in Edinburgh at Heriot-Watt University. In the early days after graduation, they kept in touch by letter, then email, and latterly, with Facebook. In 1992, I made friends with an American woman, Elina Milano, through our mutual interest in the Camino de Santiago de Compostela. At that time, I was interested in walking The Way, since reading about it in *The Pilgrimage* by Paulo Coehlo. Although it seemed rather unlikely that I would be fit enough, mentally or physically, to make this journey, I was able to experience my own spiritual pilgrimage through my friend. When she did the Camino in July 2005, we kept in touch throughout the thirty-day walk. For some reason, our friendship developed through the daily writing about our lives. To be honest, I didn't really have too much to write about in those days. My life was fairly routine, yet she maintained the contact. I thank God every day for my friendship with her. In many ways, she was the soul connection that I needed in those years when I believed the spirit had left my body.

Some years later, we met in Dublin and visited the village where she had lived for three years. Uncannily, Elina was actually from South America. This helped me identify with the strong connection I had with Spain and the Spanish language since childhood. I often wonder why she continued our friendship, especially in those early days, when I had little to offer in return. With few contacts and my lack of employment at that time, I had no idea where I was going. Unfortunately, the way had not yet been shown to me. When she visited Scotland last year and we travelled to Liverpool, I was still in the midst of the difficult times which had haunted me.

Therefore, I believe that the Internet and social media sites are exceptional in their ability to transcend time and space. If used with good faith, there is much to be gained by finding out about people who live in different countries, especially with respect to their customs and way of life. On Facebook, I find that there has been a transformation in myself after interacting with people from all walks of life and from different compartments. For people who live their lives in these compartments, perhaps this aspect of Facebook is difficult for them as they start having to live a new truth. From my experience with Facebook, it inspires me to form a stronger identity and express myself like never before. So, as described in *Twelfth Insight: The Hour of Decision* by James Redfield, we start to talk a new truth, and hopefully this allows other people to express their true feelings. This epiphany took some years to take place, and it has taken place with the help of various mentors. It has been a time of opening and closing doors and of acceptance that some people are in your life only for a set period. With respect to Facebook, I have applied the principles of the New Thought Movement with posting songs or clips from uplifting films.

Now I believe that I have attained the place of peace in my life whereby I no longer want or need anything other than what I have or what I am. There are no highs or lows, no feeling of needing excitement. It is a place of complete peace and fulfilment.

CHAPTER

24

Coming Home

O ver the period I was suffering from depression, my house and job became my prisons. Today, I find it hard to believe that I once felt this way. I saw darkness where there was only light. After this period, returning home was a great source of relief. I spent time at my local church; my mother and I were regulars there. I came to know some of the parishioners well enough to say hello and chat about everyday things. I used to hate going to the local Asda supermarket, but nowadays, I see it as an opportunity to meet old friends and some neighbours from the place where we used to live. Because the money was not exactly flowing, I had to spend more time at home and in the local neighbourhood.

As always in situations such as these, people, even in my family, sometimes felt that they did not want to intrude. I was still in touch with my cousin Gerard; he has supported me throughout the years, both good and bad. One day after I had been discharged from the hospital, my cousin Peter arrived at my house with a bunch of beautiful flowers. He made me feel things would improve and that he cared about my well-being. Sadly, Peter died last May from cancer; he was only fifty. As devastating as it was for us all, I learned so much from him in his life. At his funeral, so many people filled the church, and grown men cried for their loss. On that day, I realised that I wanted to emulate Peter's caring nature. When my day comes, I hope that I will pass peacefully, knowing that I touched people's lives. Time is very precious, and so often, we waste time thinking about what might have been.

When a person has a mental breakdown and ceases to function, they need someone to take the reins until they can recover and deal with their own affairs. This can take a considerable period of time, and it varies from person to person. When I became ill again almost five years ago, I was working on a nine-month contract, with five months to go. I had to terminate the contract because of the illness. Unfortunately, after my return to work, I had only been able to find contract work in different CA practices. Each of these firms expected more work for less money than I was used to receiving; it was difficult to integrate into the staff system. There was much to learn whilst coping with the workflow and meeting new clients. Because my new job was more than one hour away, I had to purchase a car. My family members were very anxious and upset naturally about having to help with the bills when I became ill.

At the time, I had little money to socialise, and I found it difficult to go into Glasgow on my own on the train. More than five years have passed since I last socialised at night in

Glasgow on my own. You know, even though I no longer miss it, I suppose that sometimes I feel older than my years because of this experience. Slowly, I started to find an interest in the local people around me. As a result, my mind healed, allowing me to start trusting people again.

I believe that no man is an island and that a strong sense of community is necessary for the survival of each person. From the cradle to the grave, each person should be treated with respect and dignity, irrespective of their race, religion, social position, or intelligence. This should be taught in the schools and in the prisons. People need a sense of belonging and acceptance in order to be themselves.

Abraham Maslow's Hierarchical Needs pyramid explains to us that once our basic needs are met, we then start to look for higher-order fulfilments. Some homeless people do not have the luxury of reading Plato or Socrates. There is not enough being done to alleviate the stress these people have to endure. The fate of some of the elderly people who end up in nursing homes because their children can't afford to take care of them is heartrending. This tragedy is a sign of our times. Many of these people are neglected in these homes, and they are unable to tell about their stories because of their Alzheimer's illness. If the human race is going to survive another century, we will have to change our ways and employ empathy towards our fellow man.

A person should never suffer from depression alone in our world. This is an opportunity for us to appreciate the benefits to being alive and to support our friends and family. If you were to live to one hundred years of age, it would be impossible to experience everything the world has to offer. I was the classic person who kept my problems to myself. Due to the fact that I had not dealt with these problems at the time, they manifested themselves in three breakdowns. A pressure cooker is an apt illustration of how my life was building to a point of no return. Funnily enough, when I went to Glasgow University, I wanted to leave my hometown. Yet I used to go to the local nightclub there, even during my degree. I think everyone felt the same way when we all joined hands for the last song, "New York, New York" by Frank Sinatra, in which he talks about the "little town blues" (Ebb and Kander 1980).

The conclusion is that the grass is often greener on the other side. It's too easy to forget what is important in life.

For some years, I considered my home to be a prison, yet the period of solitude gave me the time to read, watch movies, and contemplate my future. My family supported me through this period, financially and emotionally. Sometimes we build our own prisons; surrounded by a fortress which prevents people from coming too close.

I found that the town and the people with whom I lived had not changed in the time I had neglected it. Meeting old friends from school and finding out about their lives gave me a renewed sense of self.

The Good Life

I love Tony Bennett's "The Good Life". Only recently, I bought my first CD of his *The Duets*. At eighty-four, this amazing man is still travelling the world selling out stadiums. He's a great inspiration to us all. The song talks about what makes a good life. To be honest, it seems too simple and straightforward, but I still love it.

When I was younger and more affluent, I considered most of this advice to be what I would follow when I advanced in years. The old adage of "work, rest, and play" is actually the most important concept that we ever need to use in our lives. All three are essential for our good mental health and for us to function at optimum level.

The emphasis on having fun in the song is what I would like to discuss now. Sometimes in our lives, having fun seems to be something that happens to everyone else. I believe that happiness comes from within, and that it is possible to remain in this state irrespective of what happens to you in your life. We are merely passing through this world; it is necessary to transcend time in order to be freed from the suffering that sometimes surrounds us. It is not a matter of being detached from the people that you love; detachment is a coping mechanism which is essential to prevent increased or decreased mood states.

Family is important, as is having someone to love you. This doesn't necessarily need to be love in a romantic sense. Just the experience of feeling loved makes all the difference in the world. To give love in return is an amazing experience. To find your passion is essential. This is, of course, different for everyone, and it is a unique experience to find the secret of what makes you happy. Some people search all of their lives and spend vast sums of money to find it, whilst others realise very quickly that it is a song, a poem, or perhaps the boy next door who makes them happy.

For me, the good life is when you feel close to joy most of the time. Small things can make you happy. As I read about in Paulo Coelho's *The Alchemist: A Fable,* sometimes we have to travel far and wide to find the elixir of youth, only to realise upon our return that what we were looking for was actually in our own backyard. In my life, I have been fortunate to have the security and variety from having a large extended family. When we were young, there were many celebrations, weddings, christenings, and many funerals as the upper tier started to pass on.

Looking back over my life, it could have all been so different. At times, I let things slide when I should have spoken up. I was always good at standing up for the underdog and for my rights, but sometimes, being forthright is not always the answer.

Perhaps now I see why Mahatma Gandhi was so successful with his passive resistance. There is much to be said for being in the flow of existence and resisting the universal plan less. I suppose my philosophy has changed because I now believe that only certain people are meant to be in our lives. Therefore, although we may love someone and would like for them to share our life, sometimes this is not the plan of God or the universe.

The good life to me is having many friends, but also having someone special whom you love more than all of these people combined in the past, present, and future. Some people never realise what difference they make to your life, and it is difficult to share that if they do not feel the same way. When I was younger, I liked people to look a certain way. Like everyone else, I suppose I was influenced by my peers about whom to date. But the truth is that life changes, and we realise that the person we love the most is the one who walks beside us in good and bad times. So I thank this person for listening, for caring, and for not judging my life. I believe that he came into my life when I needed a friend to help me through the most traumatic years of my life. Sadly, some friends disappeared in that time, but I realise now that this was the way that God intended for my life to progress. Some people have to leave to create a space for those well-intentioned friends who can help us move forward.

Today's celebrity culture seems rather sad and tired now. Knowing which celebrities are in love seems irrelevant in the scheme of things. I attend Mass at the Church of Holy Trinity and All Saints. On All Saints Day (31 October 2012), the priest reflected on the saints who walk beside us throughout our lives, who gain little recognition from the world. Our parents, grandparents, aunts, and uncles, it is to these people we should pray and ask for assistance because it is our family who cares the most.

CHAPTER

Lifted

The Lighthouse Family's song "Lifted" has been extremely important to me over the years (Tucker, Baiyewu and Brammer 1995). The shadows were the place I lived, and it was very sad to live there. For more years than I care to remember, I lived in the darkness. I was very isolated. My belief in God helped me through the turbulent years, but sometimes, the obstacles were so great that it was too challenging to even think of the future. The Pierces have a song called "Glorious", in which they mention experiencing the "presence of God" as they knelt down to pray (Levy 2011). Although my father would say that it was an accident that we were here at all, life is a miracle from the outset. I believe that we are sent here to do good work and to make a difference to the lives of those around us.

We had many challenges in those days. However, there were many good people too, whose names I have forgotten. But if I see them at church or in town, they will still say hello or spend some time talking about the old days. They still turn out

132

for funerals too. I grew up in a strong community; I am grateful that I lived in that neighbourhood because it moulded me into the person I am today.

It was difficult being in the local hospital when my sister was a teacher in the community, as some of the patients or nursing staff knew her. I suppose we never knew the extent of how much people knew about what happened to me, but few people have ever asked me about this. So, my sister's life and my own became intertwined as she supported me through some dark days. Recently, I read something that said that sometimes you are the light at the end of the tunnel and that did make me feel different.

Several events have taken place which have convinced me of the preccence of God. In times of deep despair, I did often think that it would be perhaps better if I was no longer in this world. Sometimes I even contemplated how my demise would affect those closest to me. After Lourdes, I never thought that way again.

I asked a priest once about how I could continue when my life was so difficult, He told me something that was difficult to accept at the time. He said that despair was a mortal sin.

Prayer is the greatest gift we have been given. In this month of October, it is more important than ever to say the Rosary as it is the month dedicated to Our Lady.

PART IV

Moving Forward

CHAPTER

All Things Must Pass

Historically, in our Western society, people suffering from mental-health problems have been subjected to inhumane acts. Originally thought to be possessed by spirits and involved in witchcraft, they were sometimes imprisoned or burned at the stake in medieval times. Even since the fields of medicine and psychology were established, people have been lobotomized and locked in asylums for the rest of their days. Young women who have had children outside marriage were confined to these institutions or forced to work in convents to atone for their sins. Since the introduction of atypical, antipsychotic medications, many people have had a better life. Some others have had extreme reactions and taken their own lives.

The uniqueness of one's life experience determines whether a person will lead a fulfilled life. Many events in a person's life could be the turning points to bring about change. Unemployment, loneliness, and many other situations can cause a person to feel that their life is not worth living. There should be systems in place to make it easier for these people to ask for this help without being made to feel weak or marginalised by society. For every homeless person we see, there is a story. Perhaps, he once had a home and a family, but something happened to him, which prevented him from staying in his place of safety. Current campaigns do not even expose the tip of the iceberg. In a society in which one in four people will be affected by mental-health problems in their life, let's just admit that life can be extremely challenging at times. We need to acknowledge that sometimes people cannot cope and they need some assistance – and dignity.

As I write this chapter, the government has greatly reduced benefits for the people who are most in need of this help. It is a sad state of affairs that instead of investing in research to improve lives, the reduction of help for the most marginalised of society is taking place. This is an extremely sad situation; instead of investing money in research, education, and counselling, they prefer to continue this treatment which will shorten the lives of these people while making some people very wealthy.

In our society today, people have to work to pay for day care of their children or the care of their elderly parents in the nursing home. Others have to pay for school, for university, or exotic holidays to keep upside the Joneses.

Change is essential and now is the critical time for it to happen. We have to look to the future, to move forward to a time of better wellbeing so we can have faith in the future. Many people have come before us and tried to force change, but this time, the world is crying out for help.

Starting Over

This book ends in a good place, some five years after my last relapse. It has not been easy, and I was very lucky to meet the people I did in the last few years who helped me move forward in every aspect of my life. Some of the people who came into my life were miraculous.

I give thanks every day for meeting Lilia Sinclair, who shared her networks with me and invited me into her world of alternative health.

I also am very grateful for my immediate and extended family and friends, old and new, who helped me come to terms with the fact that my life had changed. It is essential to admit here that my life was out of balance. Since qualifying as a chartered accountant in 1994, I thought that I was on track for a life of extreme wealth and that I would only have time to mix in certain circles. I was very much married to my work. The cost of my ambition was the potential loss of everything I once considered essential to my well-being throughout my life.

My religion – and more importantly, my *faith* – has remained very important to me throughout the last fourteen years. I believe very much that God helps those who help themselves. If we look for them, we have great opportunities for growth. Some people need more help than others though, and at different times in my life, I am very happy to say that certain people have been there to assist with the burden.

On 11 October 2012, I sat my final paper in social psychology with the Open University. All going well, I will attain a good grade. I would hope to be considered competent enough to carry out research in this field. I have really changed in the three-year period since studying psychology. I look at the world with a different perspective.

In the five years since I was last ill, I have met many challenges. Yet, for some reason, these have only made me more determined to succeed. Where there once existed obstacles, I now find ways to bypass them. I have found the most challenges from trying to convince my family that I could try working again. This task has been insurmountable, and it has been difficult to even broach the subject of returning to work with them. I wish that the government and health professionals would play a greater role in supporting people like myself who do not have the emotional support for their dreams and goals.

After having breakdowns, it takes a person a long time to have the confidence to move forward in his or her life. Often, it is the people closest to them who do not want to see that in reality, their loved one has recovered and is ready to return to the world they used to live in.

So at this stage in my life, I have to say that I have no regrets about what has passed before. As a result of becoming ill, I altered the course of my life and broadened my understanding and research into how to lead a happy, fulfilled life. Prayer is the greatest gift which we have been given.

My book draws to an end just a few weeks before November 2012, when I spent time in Sorrento with my sister and my friend, Johanna. We had an unusual meeting in Sorrento with a man we had seen some years ago. We had entered one of the churches at the end of the Mass. Funnily enough, I recognised a man we thought we had seen many years ago. At the moment in the Mass when you have to shake hands with the parishioners, he turned around and shook hands with me. He then said, "Bless you" before taking one step backwards. He then spoke to us on leaving the church and told us his name. I informed him that we had seen him some years earlier near the harbour, and he thanked us.

The next night, we met and went for a coffee. He spoke about his strong faith, and I asked him if he always felt that way in his life. He told us that he had had a difficult life, but he had absolute faith in Jesus as the Son of God. Some things he said were strange, such as the promise that I would be reborn if I moved to Sorrento and that I needn't be afraid in life because I was protected. Also, reflecting on the statue of Pope John Paul in Sorrento, he spoke of the positive energy in the area. He was evidently a man of great intelligence and faith. I felt that we must have met him for a reason, whether as a catalyst for change or as a facilitator.

Strangely enough, since writing this paragraph, I have now come to the following conclusion: although I have become well known again in the CA networks, I am not sure whether it is the place for me anymore. I worked very hard to return to my career; I sacrificed much of my life in order to be there, but now, I am now more passionate about psychology than I ever was about accountancy. The type of people I have encountered in psychology are different from those one would meet in accountancy.

Perhaps, your life path and opus will be decided for you. It will be obvious to you by the fact that you want to spend the rest of your life in the company of one person or in following the career you feel benefits society or yourself. How many people force themselves to follow a path which not only needs cleared sometimes only to find that they took the wrong path altogether?

CHAPTER

Moving On

After 2008, I had a desire to change my circumstances. Initially I believed that a return to work would facilitate this change, as I would then be financially secure and able to resume my life. The inability to plan my life in the previous years had caused major anxieties for me. It was frustrating not to be able to do the things I had enjoyed previously. These frustrations were not related to status or materialism but were more about the loss of identity and being blocked from working in the field for which I was trained. Even the pursuit of lesser jobs was unfruitful.

Sometimes in the pursuit of changes, other opportunities surprisingly become available to you. It is the first step towards your goal which is often the most challenging. However, in taking action, you find yourself on a different path altogether. It was the phone call from a mentor from Jack Canfield's office which triggered change in me. Thereafter, I decided to follow a different route for a number of years in psychology. It is interesting that although we have many advisors amongst family and friends, frequently it is the advice from a stranger that instigates the most change. In the short conversations with this mentor, she offered advice which resonated with me at that time. It allowed me to believe that I could possibly take another direction, even at a mature age. I had a renewed desire to prove myself and invest my energy in a new pathway. I wanted to prove that I could compete again at an advanced level and dispel the limited thoughts placed upon me by some of the health professionals.

Despite the events of the last fourteen years, I still have a strong believe in God. I found inner peace through visiting Lourdes in France and in the Schoenstatt Shrine in Scotland. I count my blessings every day, knowing that I am in a better place than many people who have had to endure similar experiences.

I now feel that I have achieved life balance. I am content living in the present, whilst planning for the future, but never forgetting the past. It is important not to dwell on the specific events which led to the illness, but it is important to learn from the past.

Since studying psychology, I feel that I have evolved in a different way than I would have had I still been working in business. I accepted that I was unable to return to my profession; however, I have appreciated the time which I have had to follow this alternative route. It has proved invaluable. However, the financial constraints still prevent me from participating in an active social life.

Perhaps the greatest achievement to date has been the writing of *Mary's Prayer.* Reflecting back on the last fourteen years, there were intermittent periods when I was unable to concentrate to read, which had been my greatest passion since childhood. It has been a great learning experience due to the development of research skills through my study of psychology. I have already started thinking about my next project.

Based on previous experiences, I realise that it is impossible to predict the future, however I feel optimistic about my life. Sometimes there is a fork in the road and we do not know which direction to take. Often, either path could reach the destination. One road may take longer, but it is about developing patience and belief that your circumstances can change.

I would hope that *Mary's Prayer* strikes a chord with the people who read it, whether they have experienced personal illness or not. The research which I have conducted in the process of writing *Mary's Prayer* has proved that anyone could be struck down with this illness at any time in their lives. *Mary's Prayer* hopes to promote positive mental altitudes to eradicate stigma.

I hope that if the reader in conversation with me in this book recognises something in their life story which is a parallel to mine then they must speak to someone who can help them. It is important that in light of the World Health Organisation's prediction that depression will be the major illness by 2020, that we realise that medication alone is not the answer to the problem. We are all unique; therefore, it is impossible for a consultant to comprehend all of the problems a patient has had throughout their lives in such a short timeframe.

In sharing my own experiences, I would hope that other people throughout the world feel more confident to speak about their own personal stories.

Many people find themselves as outsiders in their families when they are discharged from hospital. Others are not able to be integrated into society, so my prayer is that these people who suffer in silence will be treated with respect by the health professionals and the public so they can have a better quality of life.

Mary's Prayer hopes to answer some questions and to raise awareness of the way in which people are treated, especially when little significance is given to how they feel. I would like this story to be a beacon of light to those who feel they are all at sea. Maybe it will give sufferers some relief as they realise that their quality of life could be better. Perhaps, through reading this book, some people may find the courage to challenge their health professionals and not just accept what they predict as the future capabilities of the patients. As with any illness or person, it is important not to generalise about treatment or recovery rates. Never forget that divine intervention plays its part as well.

I have changed a great deal in the last few years. Just as the caterpillar metamorphoses into the butterfly, I have left behind many of the rigid thought patterns which I once held onto so tightly.

Even within the period of writing this book, I feel that I have experienced a shift of consciousness. In some ways, I have woken up from a dream, and there is much more for me to achieve over the coming years. If you are affected by a family member's illness or you have experienced it yourself, don't give up. There is light at the end of the tunnel.

Afterword

Lena McGuinness

My sister, Mary has been courageous in confronting the many challenges and setbacks she has encountered on her path towards recovery.

I admire Mary's strength of character. The way in which she has come to terms with the realisation of what has happened to her has been remarkable. I am also impressed with how Mary dealt with the devastating impact upon her life caused by events which were outwith her control.

Despite the lengthy period when Mary was suspended in time and distanced from the life she had known previously, she was determined to rejoin that life as soon as possible. In the initial stages of ill health, she struggled with the mental and physical limitations imposed upon her by the debilitating effects of the medications. This ultimately impacted on her daily activities and caused frustration. Mary was not discouraged; she persisted in finding a way forward. She used her ingenuity to adapt to these circumstances. Mary devised strategies to assist her to overcome this temporary and sedentary lifestyle.

When my sister first became ill, I searched the bookshelves of numerous bookstores and libraries in an attempt to find books that would help me to understand the illness and provide the best support. I needed to learn quickly whilst hoping to access expert professional advice and read about the experiences of others who had previously travelled a similar path. It was difficult to find a suitable book. Without a scientific, medical, or psychological background, most books were too technical and incomprehensible to the layman.

Education is power. I needed to educate myself in order to be able to communicate with the health professionals, to understand the medical terminology, and to raise valid questions related to Mary's condition. Once certain health professionals were unable to answer the questions, Mary embarked on a quest to attain this knowledge herself through reading and professional research. Our family have always valued education as a means to finding solutions.

Mary's personal voyage led her to discover alternative therapies, a deeper renewed spirituality, a wealth of literature, scientific journals, and inspirational music. She found the answers to her personal questions and changed direction as a result of this knowledge. The healing process had started to take place, the result of which was the creation of *Mary's Prayer.* As a result of her psychological studies, the book has evolved in a different manner than originally planned. Mary has successfully underpinned her experiences with psychological theory. I hope that Mary's reflections will be able to help people who are having similar experiences.

Throughout her life, John Lennon's music has provided the soundtrack to Mary's journey, but during the difficult years, it became especially relevant. Without John's music, Mary would have been unable to understand what was happening to her. Because he had also experienced personal trials of his own in life, she identified with him. He had searched for answers through primal therapy and the expression of pain in his music helped Mary transcend this period.

I believe that it was his *Double Fantasy* album that made the most impact on Mary at a young age. The song "Watching the Wheels" always had particular significance for her through the years in the wilderness. Mary recognised the creativity of the song "Imagine" and the power of the associated visualization techniques which are prevalent in the Law of Attraction and the New Thought Movement. She believes that if we can imagine moving from the darkness towards the light, then it is possible to train the mind to travel to a place of contentment.

Therefore, beyond the artist, Mary admired John Lennon as a person and for his work as a peace campaigner. I believe that John Lennon stood for justice. He always adopted an independent objective stance. Mary has also been interested in civil rights throughout her life and she is now relentless in her campaign against stigmatization. In particular, she would like to empower people who are unable to speak for themselves and to campaign for change.

Mary has always been interested in English and in expressing herself through language. When studying for her degree in psychology, she became particularly interested in social construction theory and social psychology, which led her to consider further research into these fields to find solutions to her problems.

Mary has drawn strength from her faith during the traumatic years. Although she is a Roman Catholic and true to her own religion, Mary has embraced other faiths in the quest to extend her spiritual knowledge and to pursue the meaning of life.

Our personal pilgrimage to Lourdes, a Marian Shrine in the French Pyrenees, proved a critical turning point for both of us. Prior to the trip, Mary had just left work and was uncertain about her future. We were adrift and could not see the way forward. For some reason, Lourdes changed everything. On our personal visits to meditate at the Grotto at Massabielle, Mary saw people less fortunate than herself, those who had travelled to the shrine in the hope of a cure. While we did not find a cure there, we found something almost as healing: inner peace. We were inspired to follow a new direction which subsequently improved Mary's health.

I am proud of Mary, for sharing her story. Crafting *Mary's Prayer* has been a remarkable achievement for her. She has embarked on a personal mission to promote understanding and to help other people. In sharing her experiences, Mary hopes to liberate others from the imprisonment of their minds and to transform lives. Education is the key to raising awareness and facilitating change.

Like the inscription on the John Lennon statue in Liverpool, Mary envisions that the world would be a better place if everyone worked towards achieving peace on earth and believed in the conservation of life.

About the Author

M ary McGuinness is a Chartered accountant who is currently studying for a degree in psychology. She lives in Scotland with her family. *Mary's Prayer* is her first book.

Bibliography

Attwood, Janet Bray and Chris Attwood. *The Passion Test* 2008.

Barker, Pat. *Regeneration (Regeneration Trilogy).* Plume Books, 2013.

Bays, Brandon *The Journey: An Extraordinary Guide for Healing your Life and Setting Yourself Free* Harper Element 1999.

Beatles, Tho. "With a Little Help from My Friends". *Sgt Popper's Lonely Hearts Club Band.* Comps. John Lennon and Paul Mc Cartney. 1967.

Brooks, Garth. *Unanswered Prayers.* Comps. Patrick Alger, Garth Brooks and Larry Bastian. 1990.

Byrne, R. *The Secret.* Harper Collins, 2006.

Byrne, Rhona. *The Secret.* Simon and Shuster, 2006.

Canfield, Jack. *The Success Principles: How to Get from Where You Are to Where You Want to Be.* Element, 2005.

Joyeux Noel. Directed by Christian Carrion. Produced by Sony Pictures Home Entertainment, 2006.

Clark, Gary. *Mary's Prayer.* Virgin Records, 1987..

Cloud, Dr Henry. *The Secret Things of God: Unlocking the Treasures Reserved for You.* Howard Books, 2009.

153

Dresser, Horatio W. *A History of the New Thought Movement.* Nu Vision Publications, 2008.pp.77-86

Dwoskin, Hale. The Sedona Method Harper Element, 2005.

There's a Spiritual Solution to Every Problem. Directed by Tedd Tramaloni. Produced by Hay House, Inc. Performed by Dr Wayne Dyer, 2007.

Ebb, Fred, and John Kander. *The Trilogy: Past, Present and Future,* 1980.

The Way. Directed by Emilio Estevez. 2011.

Music and Lyrics. Directed by Mark Lawrence. Produced by Warner Home Video, 2007.

Grassic Gibbon, Lewis. *A Scots Quair.* Polygon, 2006.

Jahoda, Maria, Paul Lazarsfeld, and Hans Zeisel. *Marienthal: The Sociography of an Unemployed Community.* New Brunswick: Transaction Publishers, 2010. pp.66-77

Kerr, Jim, and Charlie Burchill. "See the Lights." *Real Life,* 1991.

PS I Love You. Directed by Richard LaGravenese, 2008.

Lennon, John. *Double Fantasy,* 1980.

_____. *Mind Games,* 1973.

_____. *Double Fantasy,* 2000.

_____. "Cold Turkey." *Shaved Fish.* 1975.

_____. "Imagine." *Imagine.* Comp. John Lennon. 1971.

_____. "Love." *John Lennon/Plastic Ono Band.* 1970.

Lennon, John, and Paul Mc Cartney. "Penny Lane." *Sgt Peppers Lonely Heart Club Band.* 1967.

Lennon, John, and Yoko Ono. Comps. John Lennon and Yoko Ono. 1980.

Levy. "Glorious." *You and I,* 2011.

Eat, Pray, Love. Directed by Ryan Murphy, 2011.

Noweles, Rick and Ellen Shipley. 1987. "Heaven is a Place on Earth"

Oates, John, Kieron Sheehy, and Clare Wood. "Theories of Development." In *Psychological Development and Early Childhood*, by John Oates, Kieron Sheehy and Clare Wood, edited by John Oates, Kieron Sheehy and Clare Wood, 49–88. Blackwell Publishing Ltd, 2005.

Ono, Yoko. *Double Fantasy.* 1980.

———. "Season of Glass." *Season of Glass.* 1981.

Aloha fron Hawaii: Deluxe Edition. Directed by Marty Pasetta. Produced by Sony BMG, 2004.

Redfield, Stephen.*The Celestine Prophecy: An Adventure.* Bantam Books, 1994.

———. *The Twelfth Insight: The Hour of Decision.* Bantam Publlshors, 2012.

Regeneration. Directed by Gillies Mackinnon, 1997.

Rice, Anne. *Called Out of Darkness: A Spiritual Confession.* Arrow, 2009.

Scott, Mike. *The Whole of the Moon,* 1985.

The Beatles. *In My Life.* Comps. John Lennon and Paul McCartney, 1965,

Tolle, Eckhart. *The Power of Now: A Guide to Spiritual Enlightenment.* Hodder Paperbacks, 2001.

Tucker, Paul, Tunde Baiyewu, and Martin Brammer. "Lifted." *Ocean Drive,* 1995.

Vitale, Joe. *The Key: The Missing Secret for Attracting Anything You Want.* John Wiley and Sons, 2009.

Wattles, Wallace D. *The Science of Getting Rich.* Joshua Books, 2007.

August Rush. Directed by Kirsten Sheridan, 2008.

Further Reading

Cheney,Terri. *Manic.*New York: Harper Element, 2008.

Coelho,Paolo. *The Witch of Portobello.* Harper Collins, 2007.

Coelho, Paolo. *The Alchemist: A Fable about Following* Your Dream. Harper Collins, 2012.

Coelho Paolo. *The Zahir : A Novel of Obsession.* Harper Collins, 2005.

Coelho Paolo. *The Pilgrimage: A Contemporary Quest for Ancient Wisdom.* Harper Collins, 2003.

Coelho Paolo. *By the River Piedra I sat down and wept.* Harper Collins, 1999.

Dwoskin, Hale. *The Sedona Method.* Harper Element, 2005.

Gilbert, Elizabeth. *Eat, Pray, Love : One Woman's Search for Everything.* London and Bloomsbury Publishing Plc, 2006.